Elizabethan Religious Policy

Peter Holmes

Advanced
Topic*Master*

Series editors
Nicolas Kinloch
Seán Lang

Acknowledgements

The author's thanks are due to Seán Lang, Nicolas Kinloch, Philip Cross and Penny Fisher for their help and support in the production of this book.

Philip Allan Updates, part of the Hodder Education Group, an Hachette Livre UK company, Market Place, Deddington, Oxfordshire OX15 0SE

Orders

Bookpoint Ltd, 130 Milton Park, Abingdon, Oxfordshire OX14 4SB
tel: 01235 827720
fax: 01235 400454
e-mail: uk.orders@bookpoint.co.uk
Lines are open 9.00 a.m.–5.00 p.m., Monday to Saturday, with a 24-hour message answering service. You can also order through the Philip Allan Updates website: www.philipallan.co.uk

© Philip Allan Updates 2007

ISBN 978-1-84489-631-8

Impression number   5   4   3   2   1

Year   2011   2010   2009   2008   2007

Cover photograph reproduced by permission of TopFoto

Printed in Spain

Philip Allan Updates' policy is to use papers that are natural, renewable and recyclable products and made from wood grown in sustainable forests. The logging and manufacturing processes are expected to conform to the environmental regulations of the country of origin.

P01099

Contents

Introduction

The reign of Elizabeth I was an age of dynamism and nostalgia. It witnessed, as a direct result of the queen's personal policy decisions, the decisive and final triumph in England of Protestantism. As a consequence, England is still officially a Protestant country and the present Queen Elizabeth is still the Governor of the Church of England. At the same time, much of the social life of the medieval Catholic Church was swept away forever. The great demand from the intellectual and political elite was for reformation: Protestants wanted to establish an independent, national Church with a uniform service covering the whole country; Puritans wanted the church to be fully reformed; Catholic leaders also cried out for reformation.

In an age of dynamic change, there was also in Elizabethan England a strong strain of nostalgia for the past, which reached even to the upper classes, including the royal court. This becomes clear when reading Shakespeare: we enter a world of fairies, ghosts, friars and nuns, of chivalry and sword-play. But Shakespeare should not be mistaken for a Catholic; he knew what his largely Protestant audience wanted. Elizabeth clung to her old medieval oaths and, in an age when naval gunnery saved England from the Spanish Armada, to her tournaments and jousting. As a result, Elizabethan religious policy was always a little ambiguous and hesitant, and perhaps as a result too it had by the end of her reign achieved more or less what the queen had wanted.

In this book we look first at how historians have recently analysed the religious policy of the reign: broadly speaking there have been two approaches, one dynamic and the other nostalgic. In Chapter 2, we turn to Elizabeth's inheritance, both personal and political. The third chapter examines the famous religious 'settlement' of 1559, where some aspects of Elizabeth's religious policy were first unveiled in the year following her accession. Chapters 4 and 5 look at how a Puritan movement developed during the reign, trying to push Elizabeth into further reformation. We then turn to the Catholic response to Elizabeth's policy in Chapter 6. In Chapter 7 there is an analysis of Elizabeth's developing anti-Catholic policy. Finally, in Chapter 8, there is an attempt to evaluate Elizabeth's policy by looking at what she had achieved, and what she had failed to do by the end of her reign in 1603.

Terms defined in the glossary are highlighted in purple the first time they appear in each chapter for easy reference.

Peter Holmes

What is the standard view of historians on the Elizabethan Reformation?

In the last generation history writing on the English Reformation has undergone a dramatic change, to such an extent that we cannot talk confidently even now about a 'standard view' on the topic. Historians have disagreed and continue to disagree. The effect this may have on the poor students who are asked to study the period is likely to be rather a bewildering one: if the historians cannot agree, what are the students supposed to think? So, the commonest student error is probably that of taking the broad interpretations of the period offered by the historian being read at the time as somehow beyond criticism. Since historians disagree among themselves, there is room for intelligent students to evaluate the theories and generalisations and come to their own conclusions, as long as there is evidence to support them.

Periodisation: the place of Elizabeth I's reign in the English Reformation

One of the most difficult problems facing historians is periodisation: how should we divide time into periods? This book uses the standard division provided by the reign of a ruler, in this case Elizabeth I, 1558–1603. This is clearly sensible if the focus is on the policy of one monarch, but less useful if we are also dealing — as we should be — with the religious life of the country as a whole, which to some degree follows a pattern and rhythm of its own. It is generally agreed that the religious history of Elizabeth I's reign must be set against the background of what is called the Reformation, which began in about 1529, although even this date is open to debate. So perhaps it is wrong to barge into the story of the Reformation in 1558 when we should really begin 30 years earlier. It is also possible to argue that there was an important turning point in Elizabeth's religious affairs that falls in the middle of the reign, so the year 1580 might be a more important dividing line than either 1558 or 1603. In the end, though, we might conclude that the historian has to divide things up somehow, and the reign of Elizabeth I was quite long enough to establish some valid historical generalisations without needing to go outside it.

What might be called the standard view of how to periodise English religious history in the sixteenth century was that offered by A. G. Dickens in his textbook, first published in 1964, entitled *The English Reformation*. Dickens began his discussion with the Lollards, a religious group who first appeared in the late fourteenth century, but his book really gets going in the 1520s. The bulk of the discussion covers the years from the fall of Wolsey (1529) to the death of Queen Mary (1558). Elizabeth I's reign is dealt with by Dickens in just 36 pages out of 463, in a sort of postscript, making broad points that spill out into the next century and with none of the detailed narrative of the earlier pages. According to Dickens the English Reformation was concluded with Elizabeth's accession and the settlement of 1559. For Dickens, Elizabeth I's reign was a period of consolidation that revealed the problems implicit in the earlier reformation, but contributed little more to what had already been achieved in the earlier 'heroic' period of religious change. What mattered for him was the rapid change from Catholicism to Protestantism, which the events of the 1530s and 1540s ushered in. By the time of Elizabeth's accession this had been achieved and her role was to overturn the efforts of her predecessor, Mary I (1553–58), who destroyed what had been achieved under Henry VIII and Edward VI. According to Dickens, the settlement of 1559 was a 'revolution' because it turned things round, back to where they had been before Mary came to the throne. However, this revolution was the end of the period of reformation in England. Dickens uses the word 'denouement' twice to describe Elizabeth I's reign: the denouement of a play is the final scene in which the problems set out earlier in the drama are unravelled and solved.

In fact, Dickens was too good a historian not to see that such an approach undervalues the religious events of Elizabeth I's reign and he was good enough a scholar to admit that there was a second 'reformation' in the Civil War and Restoration period 1640–88, when many of the achievements of the years 1529–59 were radically altered. However, this only served to emphasise that the years 1559–1640 were rather a boring period, outside the main drama. There is something to be said, of course, for Dickens's view. It is very helpful to think about an English Reformation in the reigns of Henry VIII and Edward VI by which England changed from Catholicism to Protestantism, especially if one realises that there was a second one a century later. Indeed, one way or another later historians have often followed this periodisation, which in any case was not original to Dickens. Thus, Dr Eamon Duffy, in other respects a great critic of Dickens, finished his well-known counter-history of the Reformation, *The Stripping of the Altars*, in 1570 and is almost as terse as Dickens on the reign of Elizabeth I — although it is only fair to add that Duffy's book was already extremely long.

Dickens is therefore often accused, perhaps unfairly, of supporting the view that the English Reformation was a short affair. Critics who attack this view suggest that religious change was by no means complete by 1559 and that the 'long reformation' continued through Elizabeth I's reign and into the Stuart period. Hence, later religious histories of this period, for example the one by Claire Cross in the 1970s and the more recent history by Peter Marshall, cover a much longer period than Dickens. This longer focus does on the whole seem better, and it helps rescue Elizabeth's religious history from oblivion. It might also help resurrect the so-called 'Whig' interpretation of events, which G. R. Elton tried hard to resist, that held that there might be a link between Dickens's first and second reformations and that the origins of the religious changes of the Stuart period can be found in Elizabeth I's reign. The most prominent revisionist sixteenth-century historian, that is the one keenest to revise the Dickens standard view, is Christopher Haigh, who entitled his 1993 book *English Reformations*, using the plural. He wished to suggest that there were a number of religious changes in the century, all equally valid and worthy of study. Haigh argued that to focus, as Dickens did, on a Protestant Reformation, which started in 1529 and achieved its denouement in 1559, was to ignore the significance both of the Marian Catholic Reformation and of the very important developments of other reigns. If we apply this idea to the reign of Elizabeth I, we find that there were highly significant changes to Catholicism and even to Protestantism, and any historian of sixteenth-century religion would be wrong to ignore them or to deny them the status of reformation. So from Dickens's two reformations we have now moved to multiple reformations, even without going beyond 1603.

Reformation from below or from above?

Another point of controversy among historians is whether the religious changes of the sixteenth century were imposed on the people by the Crown (reformation 'from above' or 'top down'), or whether they arose out of a popular desire for change ('from below' or 'bottom up'). On the face of it, this looks like a pointless question: quite obviously the Reformation was an act of state, the result of royal decisions made by the Tudors, who used parliament, the representative assembly of the nobility and the richer members of the community, to impose their choice of religion on the rest of the population. There might be an interesting debate to be had about how important the monarch was in the decision-making process in relation to the Lords and Commons, but whatever the case, it was an act of state. Elizabeth I's reign is no different because everyone agrees that the big decisions on religion were made in the parliament that the queen called at the very beginning of her reign. However, for A. G. Dickens and the Protestant school of historians that followed him, the answer lay a bit deeper than that. Dickens felt that there was an influential movement of support for the Reformation among the people of England, which grew out of a strong feeling of dissatisfaction with the abuses of the medieval Church. This movement from below was what made the Tudors' act of state acceptable to the population. In the reign of Elizabeth I the momentum continued so that, while the queen's settlement of 1559 was greeted with general approval, its moderation stirred up the opposition tendency, which became known as Puritanism. According to Patrick Collinson, whose *Elizabethan Puritan Movement* appeared in 1967 and followed the same broad lines as Dickens, Puritanism was a 'movement'. 'Movement' was very much a mid-twentieth-century word, used to describe grass-roots political groups like the early Labour Party. So, according to this standard view, the development of Protestantism in Elizabeth I's reign was not envisaged or encouraged by the queen; as well as the act of state the actions of the people mattered.

With the appearance of J. J. Scarisbrick's *The Reformation and the English People* in 1983 there started a Catholic backlash against the Dickens view of the Reformation as a popular, almost natural, response to the corruption of the Catholic Church. Scarisbrick's period also ended in 1559, but his central point was applicable to some degree to the rest of Elizabeth I's reign. He showed that there was far more in late medieval Catholicism that commanded respect than Dickens had allowed for, and that there was solid evidence for the popularity of many aspects of the late medieval Church. This message was reiterated by Eamon Duffy's *The Stripping of the Altars* (1992), which said much the same as Scarisbrick, though at far greater length. The historian who applied this 'revisionist' approach (as he himself was fond of calling it) to the reign of Elizabeth I most successfully was Christopher Haigh in *English Reformations*. According to Haigh, Elizabeth I inherited a country in which many areas were still committed to Catholicism; nonetheless, she used her position as queen to impose a Protestant settlement. Even by the end of her long reign this new religion had failed to convert the whole country, despite the best efforts of Protestant propagandists and the use of force against Catholic dissidents.

How popular was the Elizabethan Reformation across the country?

Old religious rivalries have been played out in the struggle over English Reformation history: the Catholics, Scarisbrick and Duffy, against the Protestants, Dickens and Collinson. Haigh's 'religion' is revisionism, a desire to turn old theories on their heads: as a result he has tended to side with the Catholics, who stood against the tide of earlier academic discussion, although there is a much older Catholic tradition of history-writing to which they could appeal. For the Catholic or the revisionist historian, the Reformation was a long drawn-out affair, imposed on a reluctant population by a self-seeking nobility and monarchy. Even by 1603 this process was hardly complete; the best the monarch could hope for was the acquiescence of a conformist, apathetic population, the majority of whom were illiterate. For the Protestant historian, the Reformation was popular at first among a dynamic section of the community who made common cause with those Tudors who had the sense to see what would be both personally beneficial and also acceptable to the people. Dickens and Collinson admitted that it took some time to convert the mass of the people to the new religion, but by 1603 this had been largely achieved and opponents were in a tiny minority. Thus, the central controversy turns on the key question: how much popular support did the Reformation command? In the modern age of democracy this would provide the answer to the deeper philosophical, but perhaps not historical, question: was the Reformation good or bad for the country?

One reason for this central dilemma is that the evidence that can be used to answer it is difficult to handle, and this may explain the difference of opinion between respected historians. The sources for social history are hard to interpret. The evidence can be anecdotal, based on the subjective views of a contemporary whose writings have come down to us. A large part of the material used in social history relies on records of law courts, which tend to exaggerate the prevalence of nonconformity. Great weight is attached to wills and the religious language they contain, but it seems clear that most wills were written not by the testator but by someone else, generally a clergyman, so they are not necessarily good evidence for the religious beliefs of the laity. Much of the most interesting work on sixteenth-century religious history has been in local history: Dickens himself was a historian of Lollardy and Catholic recusancy in Yorkshire and Haigh studied Lancashire, a strongly Catholic area. These local studies can help to illuminate the question of what the people felt about religious change. However, they also show the diversity and complexity of religious belief within the relatively small compass of an English county and, more importantly, across the country as a whole. What was popular in rural Lancashire was often less to the taste of people in Hull or even in nearby Manchester. The more the social history of the English Reformation is studied the more complex the picture becomes.

Elizabethan religious history is therefore at present quite a lively field. There is also much detailed research to be done, especially in local history but also in analysing the vast output of the printing press. The work of synthesising these new detailed studies continues and may be said to be entering a post-revisionist phase, where the two opposing camps are to some degree reconciled. These synthesisers are best represented by Diarmaid MacCullough and Peter Marshall. MacCullough, historian of Tudor Suffolk, a strongly Protestant county, may perhaps have more sympathy with Dickens and the pre-revisionists, but his *The Later Reformation in England, 1547–1603* can be relied upon to present a balanced survey. Peter Marshall has surveyed almost two centuries of religious history in his *Reformation England 1480–1642* (2003), which presents an overview of recent research and walks a sensible middle way between the extremes of the pre- and post-revisionist approaches.

This overview of the current debates among historians on Elizabeth I's religious history might be rather daunting for a student who is looking for a pathway through what seems to be a bit of a jungle. It is therefore worth repeating what the great issues are here, so readers may try to arrive at a balanced opinion of them as they read on. First, was the Reformation over by 1558, or did Elizabeth I's reign contribute some significant developments? Second, were the religious events of Elizabeth I's reign entirely the result of her policy or were other forces involved? Third, how popular was Elizabeth's religious policy, both at the beginning and the end of her reign? Fourth, following on from the last point, what did the map of religious beliefs in Elizabeth I's reign look like? It will be these broad themes that are discussed in more detail in the chapters that follow.

Questions

1 At what point can a reformation be said to have been achieved or ended?
2 What does the debate about reformation 'from above' or 'from below' reveal about the relationship between religious belief and lay authority in the Tudor period?
3 What are the advantages and disadvantages of local studies in analysing religious belief in Tudor England?

What was Elizabeth I's religious inheritance?

When Elizabeth I came to the throne in 1558, she inherited both a problem and its solution. The bulk of this chapter examines the problem and at the end we will look briefly at Elizabeth's solution. In view of how important it is to put Elizabeth I's reign in the wider context of the English Reformation, it is necessary to spend some time on what happened before she came to the throne and also to look briefly at what she inherited from continental Europe. Throughout the sixteenth century, English religious life was profoundly influenced by currents of thought coming across the English Channel. Indeed, it often looks as though the English were incapable of developing their own theological ideas and were reliant on influences from abroad. Even when the English did develop their own religious ideas, it was often when they were forced to travel abroad.

The influence of the Reformation in Europe

The religious problem for Elizabeth I was the same as that faced by her two predecessors, Edward VI (1547–53) and Mary I (1553–58) — that the country was divided in religion and it was the job of a ruler to give some leadership on how the religious life of the country was to be conducted. This was a new challenge: when Henry VIII (1509–47) had come to the throne it was almost universally accepted, first, that England was a Catholic country and second, that the king had no authority to make major religious decisions for the people. This all changed in the years following 1517.

The most important event to affect the history of England in the sixteenth century occurred not in England but in Germany, when in October 1517 an obscure Augustinian monk called Martin Luther pinned 95 Theses — academic points for debate — on the door of the university church in Wittenberg. From this event developed what has become known as the Protestant Reformation. Luther's reformation was rapid and devastating, sending shock waves all over Europe. Before Luther the Catholic Church had held sway over western Europe more or less for as long as it had been Christian, in some places for more than 1,000 years. There had been influential heretics who had led movements of opposition to the Church, most notably the Englishman John Wycliffe and the Bohemian (Czech) Jan Huss, but their supporters had all been crushed or driven underground. Luther drew on the ideas of these forerunners while rejecting the more extreme views of other heretics. The difference was that he succeeded where they had failed. The Protestant Reformation attacked the Roman Catholic Church in four interrelated areas: church government, the role of the clergy in society, religious belief or doctrine and how to conduct church services.

On the question of who was to run the Church, Protestants rejected the leadership of the pope. The bishops of Rome had established a sometimes precarious leadership over the western European church, and for years their position had been questioned in three ways. First, it was clear that many of the men who became popes were not fit for the job, living irreligious lives of immorality in conspicuous luxury. This was satirised in the writings of the Dutch humanist scholar Desiderius Erasmus, whose work did much to prepare the way for Luther, though he himself remained a Catholic. Second, the papacy made financial and political demands on the laity and clergy all over Europe, which were increasingly resented, especially by ambitious kings, princes and noblemen. Luther's 95 Theses were inspired by the arrival in Germany of an indulgence seller, sent there by the pope to raise money by selling certificates that claimed to forgive the sins of those who purchased them, the money being destined to finance the building of the Basilica of St Peter's in Rome, to gratify the megalomania of a particularly greedy pope. Third, the Protestant attack on the papacy was broadened into a wider attack on the role of the clergy as a whole in society. After all, if papal leadership was questioned, why should the power of bishops and even priests and monks be immune from attack? Most obviously in the firing line were the rich and corrupt monasteries (corrupt in the sense that they did not practise the rules of poverty laid down by their founders). Luther, as a monk, had direct knowledge of such corruption. He believed that every person had the capacity to be his or her own priest, either by reading the Bible or by accepting the word preached by those who could read. He made a very practical demonstration of these beliefs by renouncing his own monastic vows, marrying a former nun and translating the New Testament from Latin, the language of the clergy, into German, the language of the people.

Luther and his followers had already challenged Catholic beliefs radically by their stance on authority within the Church, but Luther was to challenge beliefs in even more fundamental ways when he developed his teaching on 'justi-fication', or what was needed to get to heaven. Lutherans rejected the Catholic orthodoxy that people were justified (saved) by their 'works': attendance at Mass and other Catholic religious services and charitable or hospitable actions. According to Luther's view, which revived an old Catholic tradition, people were justified by their faith — by what they *believed* rather than by what they *did*. Luther's onslaught on indulgences was accompanied by the wholesale rejection of the concept of purgatory, which underpinned the idea that prayers for the dead provided a route into heaven. Lutherans also challenged beliefs on the nature of religious services. According to the Catholic Church, religious ceremonies, conducted by a special caste of priests, were key events in Christians' progress to salvation. Luther was keen to stress the role of the laity and to reduce that of the clergy. He denied that there were seven sacraments, accepting only two: Communion and baptism. He rejected the Catholic belief in auricular confession, the one-to-one discussion between priest and penitent. In the Communion service Luther also questioned the Catholic doctrine of transubstantiation, which taught that the bread and wine actually became the body and blood of Christ when the priest blessed them. Other reformers who followed him completely abandoned any belief in the physical presence of the body and blood in the bread and wine and said that Communion was simply a commemoration of Jesus's Last Supper. Luther was unwilling to go so far and accepted 'consubstantiation', a sort of halfway house between Catholic and radical views that did not completely deny the actual presence of Christ in the bread and wine. Lutherans also fundamentally modified Catholic practice by allowing Communion 'in both kinds' (both bread and wine) for the laity as well as for the clergy. Catholic priests only gave the laity the bread.

The Protestant Reformation initiated by Luther developed a fresh momentum when it arrived in Switzerland in the 1520s. Ulrich Zwingli in Zurich and, in the next generation, John Calvin in Geneva, emerged as the great leaders of the Reformation. Both were to have a huge influence in England.

Henry VIII

It was these religious reforms that presented the theological problems that faced Catholic England in the years after 1517. Luther's ideas spread quickly in Germany and spilled over into the neighbouring countries of western Europe. By the early 1520s the Lutheran Reformation had produced a profound effect on a small group of English clergy, academics and urban laymen, especially in two influential places, the University of Cambridge and the City of London. These early English Lutherans, called 'evangelicals' by historians, began to preach, write and agitate in favour of an English reformation. Their leading figure was William Tyndale, who translated the Bible into English, using Luther's

German translation to help him, and wrote a book calling on Henry VIII to lead his kingdom into a rejection of the pope and into wholesale secularisation of the immense wealth of the Church. However, the king's first response was to persecute Lutherans. In 1521 Henry VIII, with help from Sir Thomas More, wrote a book condemning Luther and was rewarded with the title 'Defender of the Faith' by the pope.

In a period of intense political and religious activity between 1529 and 1536, however, Henry VIII executed a bewildering U-turn, accepting a large part of Luther's agenda and starting the process that we know as the English Reformation. He took three main steps. First and foremost, he rejected the authority of the pope over the Catholic Church in England: this was the famous 'break with Rome'. Using parliament to help him, Henry VIII passed the Act of Supremacy in 1534 by which he, as king, was declared to be the 'Supreme Head, under Christ, of the Church in England'. This ended the jurisdiction of the pope over England, which dated back to the seventh century. All taxes sent to Rome were taken over by the king and the right of appeal from the church courts to Rome was abolished. The king now had the power to appoint all bishops and to control the work of the clergy. England was separated from the rest of the Catholic Church. Second, Henry VIII dissolved the English monasteries, again by Acts of Parliament, passed in 1536 and 1539. There were 600 monasteries and nunneries, occupied by about 9,000 monks and nuns and owning a huge amount of property all over the country. Third, Henry VIII allowed a series of religious changes that made tentative steps towards the evangelical programme of reformation. There was an English translation of the Bible and the adoption of a number of new statements of belief, although these tended to be contradictory. The most significant Catholic doctrines to be rejected were those of purgatory and pilgrimage. The dissolution of the monasteries had been accompanied by the removal of Catholic shrines and by a wave of iconoclasm — the destruction of images, statues and pictures associated with places of pilgrimage. However, Henry VIII did not allow one major change: church services remained in Latin.

Why did Henry VIII do this? The process started with the break with Rome, which was in large part a consequence of his desire for an heir to whom he could pass on the throne of England, thus avoiding a disputed succession. Henry VIII had one child, Mary, by his wife Catherine of Aragon, but there had been no female ruler in England for 400 years, and Catherine seemed to be barren. Henry wished to divorce Catherine and marry Anne Boleyn, by whom he felt sure — erroneously, as it turned out — he would have a son. However, the ultimate decision on whether or not he could divorce Catherine lay with the pope, who was in the political control of Catherine's nephew, the Emperor

Charles V, who opposed the divorce. So there seemed to be no alternative to the break with Rome, simply in order to divorce Catherine. However, there was no need for such a breach in relations with the papacy to be permanent; the fact that it was made so shows that Henry VIII and the political elite in England had accepted a large part of the Lutheran belief that papal and clerical power was not legitimate, whereas that of kings and other lay rulers was. The desire for money and power was also a significant motive both in breaking with Rome and in closing the monasteries, not just from personal avarice, but out of a desire to strengthen the monarchy, preserve civil peace and defend the country from attack. Hovering over all these practical arguments for what Henry VIII did was a great movement in ideas, of which many people in England were only dimly aware but which strongly influenced the educated elite. These were the ideas, both Catholic and Lutheran, of reform — a desire to return to the original bases for Christianity, to the Bible and to a simpler ideal of religion. The nobility and gentry who took over the monasteries' lands were well aware that it had originally belonged to their own ancestors, who had given it away to the monks; they also knew that the founders of the religious orders had believed in poverty and humility.

When Henry VIII died in 1547 he left England in a sort of religious limbo, neither really Catholic nor fully Protestant. Why did the king not go all the way with Luther? First, religious life all over Europe was in a state of flux, with no clearly established template of a reformed ecclesiastical system. Second, we must assume that Henry himself did not wish to take the process too far. The ruling classes in Europe held firmly to what modern historians have labelled 'conservative' views in religion: they feared that if the reformation went too far it would stir the people into a more general revolt, not only against the Church, but also against kings and noblemen. This anxiety had surfaced in Germany where, in 1525, as a result of Luther's ideas, a major peasants' revolt broke out. Worse still, in 1533 the German city of Münster was taken over by a radical religious group, the Anabaptists, who not only reformed the church but also deposed the magistrates, instituted communism and denounced the concept of family. Henry VIII wanted to benefit from religious reform, not be deposed as a result of it, so he was responsive to conservative arguments that the reformers should be kept in check. However, there was also danger from the other side of the religious divide. In 1536 there occurred the most serious rebellion in England in the whole Tudor period, the Pilgrimage of Grace. For a few months the whole of the north of England was in open revolt and York, the capital of the north, had been taken over by a rebel army. This was not just a peasants' revolt; it was supported by a large section of the nobility and gentry. Although there were economic and other non-religious reasons for the rebellion, the pilgrimage was essentially a protest against Henry VIII's religious policy and against the influence at court of reformers like Thomas Cranmer, the Archbishop of Canterbury and Thomas Cromwell, the king's secretary. The rebellion fizzled out and there were reprisals, but royal policy for the next 10 years until Henry VIII's death in 1547 was remarkably conservative. Henry did not go back on the major reforms of 1529–36, but he refused to take them any further.

Edward VI (1547–53)

Henry VIII was succeeded by his 9-year-old son, Edward VI. Religious policy during his reign was decided mainly by the adults who ruled in his name, first his uncle, the Duke of Somerset, and later the Duke of Northumberland. Both were Protestants and the boy king gave them his full support in their pursuit of further reformation. It was in Edward's reign that the English Reformation reached its high-water mark. In 1547, the chantries were abolished. These were chapels attached to many churches, where priests were employed to sing masses for the souls of the dead. The earlier attack on purgatory, implicit in the dissolution of the monasteries and places of pilgrimage, had pointed the way to this change. Once again it involved a great increase in revenue to the Crown, since the chantries owned land and property given to them by laity frightened of purgatory. There was also a loss of local amenities, especially schools, as chantry priests were often teachers linked to local confraternities and guilds. This was partially remedied by the creation of King Edward VI Grammar Schools.

Next, by the 1549 Act of Uniformity, parliament introduced the first Edwardian prayer book to replace the Latin Mass, followed in 1552 by a second and more radical prayer book. The doctrine on the Eucharist in the new prayer books was based on reformed theology, with Communion given to the laity in both kinds. The 1552 Prayer Book reflected the Zwinglian belief that the Communion service was performed in remembrance of the Last Supper, and contained no hint of the Catholic idea that Christ was physically present in the Communion bread and wine. Meanwhile, the appearance of the interior of churches changed with a second wave of iconoclasm, the removal or destruction of 'idolatrous' Catholic statues and pictures.

The whole tone of English religious life became more Protestant under Edward VI. A number of important religious leaders from Europe came to England, including Martin Bucer, Bernardino Ochino, and Peter Martyr Vermigli. Under their influence some of the more radical English reformers, such as Miles Coverdale and John Hooper, wanted the reformation to go even further.

Mary I (1553–58)

The hopes of the reformers were dashed, however, when the young king died of tuberculosis in 1553 and his elder sister, Mary, seized control in the face of strong Protestant opposition. Mary was the child of Catherine of Aragon and also a child of the Catholic Church. She threw the reformation into reverse and overturned much of what had been done by Henry VIII and Edward VI. She restored England to the Catholic Church and to obedience to the papacy. The venerable Cardinal Reginald Pole, a minor member of the royal family and opponent of the Henrician Reformation, who had been in exile in Italy since the 1530s, returned to England as Papal Legate to accept the country back into the Catholic Church in the name of the pope. As Archbishop of Canterbury, Pole directed Marian religious policy. Mary and Pole are often portrayed by Protestant historians as wild-eyed fanatics, but they were pragmatic enough to accept that the dissolution of the monasteries and chantries could not be overturned: too much of their property had been bought up by the laity and parliament would never agree. Mary did begin to re-endow monasteries herself, especially the abbey at Westminster, and she also restored a little of the revenue and property that had also been taken from the bishops under Henry VIII and Edward VI, though she was hardly generous.

Mary's best-known policy, however, was much less enlightened and less effective: she began to persecute Protestants as heretics. The Catholic Church had developed a way to deal with heretics: there was a trial and if the heretics refused to recant they were handed over to the lay authorities, who would burn them at the stake. A steady trickle of Lollards, followers of John Wycliffe, had been treated in this cruel fashion and both Henry VIII and Edward VI had burnt religious extremists as heretics. Mary's persecution of Protestant heretics was remarkable because it involved, by English standards, a relatively large number of deaths: 280, mainly in the second half of her brief reign. The executions were concentrated in areas where heresy was strongest, especially London and the southeast, so the scale of the bloodshed seemed worse to contemporaries there. In addition, leading figures from Henry VIII's and Edward VI's reigns were executed, including Archbishop Cranmer and Bishops Nicholas Ridley and Hugh Latimer. There is little question that Mary's persecution was unproductive as well as cruel: it did not stamp out heresy (although a supporter of Mary might maintain that it was not given enough time) and it helped create a myth of Catholic barbarity and Protestant courage, best shown in John Foxe's extremely popular — and highly biased — 1563 account of the persecution in his *Acts and Monuments of the English Martyrs*.

Mary also drove about 1,000 leading English Protestants into exile. These people travelled to southern Germany and Switzerland, where they were hospitably received by the followers of Zwingli and Calvin and had their beliefs confirmed and strengthened. When they came back to England after Mary's death they did so with the experience of having lived as part of thoroughly reformed congregations fresh in their minds. Once again, continental ideas were influencing the development of English religion.

Mary's reign, like Edward's, was cut short by her death. Also like Edward, Mary failed to leave an heir to carry on her work: her unpopular marriage to Philip II of Spain had produced nothing more than a phantom pregnancy. Both reigns can be judged to have been failures, largely because neither monarch lived long enough to build on what they were trying to achieve, or to put right the mistakes they had made. The 1540s and 1550s were a difficult time in economic, social, medical and diplomatic terms, and it is against this background that the two rulers had struggled. Mary died in November 1558 and left the throne to her half-sister, Elizabeth.

Religious change and the English people

This brief survey of Elizabeth I's religious inheritance has focused on the activities of monarchs and parliaments rather than on the English people. How were they affected by these religious changes? There is no clear answer to this. Clearly some people were confirmed as Catholics by the Marian restoration: historians have detected signs of a Catholic revival during her reign. Another section of the population favoured a more moderate Henrician religious solution, with some aspects of Catholic ceremonies but no interference from Rome. A third group wanted a thoroughgoing Protestant reformation; and there were also a large number of people who were essentially apathetic, either because they were not strongly religious (and there were certainly people of that sort in Tudor England) or because they had taken the philosophical view that it did not really matter which version of Christianity was followed. It is impossible to say how many people fell into each of these categories: the consensus among historians is that the large urban centres, especially London, tended to be more Protestant while more remote rural areas, especially in the north, were more Catholic. The younger generation was more likely to be Protestant, though for 5 years immediately before Elizabeth I's accession England had seen a revival of Catholicism. Social class is crucial in this discussion, since the mass of the people had little opportunity to influence events one way or the other. The aristocracy had a conservative streak, though this could make them Henricians rather than Marians. Protestantism was popular among people of the middling sort, the gentry, yeomanry and merchants, and possibly also among the literate and intellectual classes. The main point to emphasise, however, is that the country was divided and these divisions had the potential to lead to rebellion, even to civil war. Elizabeth I inherited a religious mess: a stalled Protestant reformation and an unsettling period of Catholic revival.

Elizabeth I's solution

There was little doubt about what sort of a solution Elizabeth would attempt to these problems. Elizabeth was a Protestant. It is a defensible position that by 1558 it did not really matter which course a ruler followed as long as the ruler stuck firmly to that course and did not die too soon. The English Reformation had unsettled the religious and political life of the country, and a period of certainty and clarity was needed. A Catholic historian might suggest that continuity with Mary's reign might have been useful, and that the foreign situation favoured a Catholic settlement; a Protestant historian would reply that the more advanced parts of the country, London and the south, were reformed and that the march of ideas was going in a Protestant direction. However, such pragmatic considerations did not weigh with Elizabeth: as the daughter of Anne Boleyn, she was not going to continue the religious policy of the daughter of Catherine of Aragon. Elizabeth's own inheritance, even her genes, provided her with the outlines of a solution to the religious divisions which faced her at the beginning of her reign.

The precise nature of Elizabeth I's religious opinions has been much debated by historians. This debate is important because it helps us understand the political forces that came together to form her religious policy. One straight-forward approach would be to look at her policy throughout her reign and then conclude that it was based on her ideas: we would then be able to picture Elizabeth as a moderate Protestant. However, with a little digging we can make the picture of her religious views, and hence of the religious policy of Elizabethan England, more complex. Elizabeth's birth had placed her in the Protestant camp as surely as Mary's ancestry put her among the Catholics. In order to marry Elizabeth's mother, Anne Boleyn, Henry VIII had made himself head of the Church; it was highly likely that their daughter would continue that policy. Anne herself had been a strong supporter of more advanced religious ideas and had she lived longer it is likely that she would have encouraged Henry to take his reformation further. One of Anne Boleyn's chaplains was Matthew Parker, Elizabeth's first Archbishop of Canterbury. Elizabeth's cousins on her mother's side featured prominently in her government. After Anne's execution, Elizabeth was brought up with her brother Edward in an increasingly Protestant atmosphere in which Edward seems to have developed quite radical religious views. Prominent among the formative influences on the young Elizabeth was Catherine Parr, Henry's last queen and a woman of strong reforming views. With this background and education, Elizabeth certainly ought to have been a Protestant.

However, there are two problems with this straightforward analysis. The first is that Elizabeth seems at times to have lacked any strong religious sentiment at all, which suggests that she had some sympathy with the religious outlook of her father as much as with that of her mother. She might even have sympathised with that section of the population which regarded religion with indifference; she certainly had little time for the Puritanism of those who wanted to turn their households into godly paradises. Elizabeth's language was coarse and peppered with medieval curses; she liked a good party, especially if there was dancing, and she spent a great deal on clothes and jewels. She possessed beautifully written manuscript collections of prayers, some in her own hand and possibly composed by her personally, though historians disagree on how to interpret this. To some it is evidence of a deep piety; others see such books merely as fashion accessories for a rich young lady. Elizabeth is probably best seen as conventionally religious, attending her chapel every day because this was her Christian duty, rather than because she was devout like Philip II or Mary. She had little time for religious leaders; she developed her religious policies with lay advisers, except at the end of her reign when she found in John Whitgift an Archbishop of Canterbury with whom she saw eye to eye. Her lack of religious enthusiasm appears to its best advantage in her desire to avoid religious persecution: this policy, which she struggled to maintain in the face of strong opposition, shows her to be a pragmatist, one who valued political peace more highly than religious correctness. Elizabeth was not made of the stuff of martyrs: in Mary's reign, when her position was dangerous, she conformed and attended Catholic Mass. Like any successful monarch, Elizabeth was first and foremost a politician.

The second caveat to the idea that Elizabeth was simply a Protestant is that she had a strong conservative streak. In a careful dissection of her recorded religious statements in letters and speeches, Susan Doran has shown Elizabeth to have been closer to Luther's ideas than to Calvin's — in other words she reflected the prevalent atmosphere in which she grew up. This placed her at odds with more advanced Protestants, or Puritans. However, she disagreed with Luther on the subject of the marriage of the clergy: she refused to be introduced to the wives of bishops on her royal progresses. She had to accept that the reformed clergy could be allowed to marry, though it is fair to add that marriage was a painful subject for her and she tended to be jealous of anyone marrying at all. On the subject of church ornaments she disagreed even with conservative Protestants. She insisted on having a crucifix and candles in her own chapel, which caused much controversy: there were frequent attempts to get her to remove these popish symbols and the crucifix was occasionally stolen by enraged Protestants, even, in 1570, by her own court jester, Patch. Elizabeth always had the crucifix replaced. In 1565, when the Dean of St Paul's, Alexander Nowell, gave a sermon in her presence attacking her use of such popish ornaments she silenced him, saying: 'Do not talk about that. Leave that, it has nothing to do with your subject, and the matter is now threadbare.' Her cross and candles were, however, just about acceptable to a Lutheran. Patrick Collinson has described her as 'an odd sort of Protestant' and Susan Doran has punned that she was 'an old sort of Protestant'. Odd or old, Protestant she certainly was.

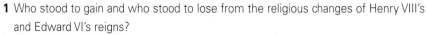

Questions

1 Who stood to gain and who stood to lose from the religious changes of Henry VIII's and Edward VI's reigns?

2 Who did more to advance the cause of Protestantism in England, Edward VI or Mary I ?

3 How important were Tudor family relationships in determining Elizabeth I's attitude towards religion?

Was the Elizabethan religious settlement accidental, and did it settle anything?

The description 'religious settlement' is a modern one and is used to describe the measures taken by Elizabeth I at the beginning of her reign to solve the religious problems she inherited. Like all historians' labels it helps us to organise a series of events in a way that makes them easier to understand. It emphasises that Elizabeth made a break from the past and that she resolved matters. The fact that we do not talk about a settlement of religion at the start of the reigns of either of her two predecessors or of the two Stuart kings who immediately followed Elizabeth I emphasises the durability of what Elizabeth achieved.

However, although in some ways useful, the term settlement is also misleading. It is associated with the way in which some historians, notably A. G. Dickens, saw the year 1559 as marking a final stage in the English Reformation and with the tendency to accord the Elizabethan settlement huge significance. Few historians today would deny that the settlement faced many challenges and widespread opposition in the 40 years that followed its introduction, yet there is still a strong desire among some commentators to argue that what was set out in 1559 gave a clear sense of direction to the religious life of the nation. According to this view, while it may not have gained universal support, the settlement did lay out clearly what the official royal line was; its opponents did at least know what they had to attack. There is something in this view, but there is also much wrong with it. The settlement developed into a continuous process, and was modified as Elizabeth's reign progressed. Even if we follow the established view and restrict our focus to the events of 1559 in this chapter, this point needs to be borne in mind.

How the settlement passed into law: was it accidental?

The chief elements of the Elizabethan settlement were very close to the religious policies adopted in the reign of Elizabeth's brother, Edward VI: Elizabeth overturned Mary's Catholic restoration and reinstated Protestantism, to some degree as Edward had left it. Royal authority over the Church was re-established by an Act of Supremacy and the liturgy was changed by an Act of Uniformity. Before looking at what these pieces of legislation did, it is necessary to look at the process by which they came to be framed and passed into law, a subject which in recent years has become something of an obsession with historians. Its interest lies in four areas: first, defining what the settlement consisted of; second, as an object lesson in how Tudor government worked; third, in helping to establish what Elizabeth's own religious ideas were; and fourth, in giving us some idea of the religious opinions in the country as a whole.

The problem in understanding how the settlement passed into law lies in interpreting the evidence available. Curiously, it is difficult to arrive at a clear solution, not because there is too little evidence but because there is too much, though of a rather fragmentary nature. The old-fashioned view, developed by the historians of the nineteenth and early twentieth centuries, was quite straight-forward: Elizabeth I came to the throne personally committed to reverting to something close to the religious situation when Edward VI died in 1553. The settlement took time to be steered through parliament but by the summer of 1559 the process was complete. Elizabeth's settlement was a little less Protestant than Edward's had been but in this it accorded with the more moderate views of the queen herself.

However, in 1954 the great biographer of Elizabeth I, Sir John Neale, published a groundbreaking article that thoroughly revised this conventional interpretation. After sifting through the evidence of what happened in Elizabeth I's first parliament, Neale, an acknowledged expert in parliamentary history, arrived at a different narrative. First, he said, Elizabeth's intention had been to produce a moderate settlement. Neale argued that she was tempera-mentally inclined to a sort of Anglicanism rather than thoroughgoing Protestantism, and in any case, she gauged the mood of the country, which also favoured moderation. She told the (Catholic) French ambassador at the very beginning of her reign that she wished to restore religion as her father left it and she assured the Spanish ambassador, another Catholic, that in matters of religion she differed little from him. There were other signs too that her religious

views were not conventionally Protestant, but when her plans for a conservative settlement were placed before parliament early in 1559, Neale claims that
they ran into strong opposition from 'Puritans' in the House of Commons, a
group of activists who had returned from exile in Geneva determined to push
through a more advanced Protestant settlement. Elizabeth had hoped that she
might balance this onslaught with support from Catholic sympathisers in the
House of Lords, but this failed because the Catholics would not support her
middle path either. When the 1559 Treaty of Cateau-Cambrésis ended the war
which had started in Mary's reign between France and the Anglo-Spanish
alliance, England was no longer threatened by Catholic attack from abroad; at
this point, in Neale's version of events, Elizabeth threw in her lot with the most
active Protestants in parliament and a more Protestant settlement than she
had initially envisaged was quickly pushed through. Thus, according to Neale,
the religious settlement of 1559 was to some degree 'accidental' (as Collinson
has described it) — the result of forces over which the queen had less control
than she might have wished. It heralded a period of intense political activity in
parliament, which thus became a prominent force, and it also helps to explain
why Elizabeth continually had to engage in a struggle with the Puritans: after
their victory in the parliamentary struggles of 1559 they were keen to achieve
even more and Elizabeth was determined not to show such weakness again.

From soon after its publication, Neale's thesis attracted some scepticism, but
it was not until the 1980s that his views were fully challenged, in a work by
Norman L. Jones, whose alternative account of what happened in parliament
has achieved something like orthodoxy. Jones in effect revived the previous
account of the settlement. Using the same sources as Neale, he argued that
Elizabeth's plans were largely achieved: she was a moderate Protestant and her
settlement was moderately Protestant too. Jones argued that the Puritan group
in the parliament of 1559 was quite small (probably 19 returned exiles sat in
the Commons) and most of them were so pleased to have a Protestant monarch
that they were not inclined to rock the boat. The impact of foreign events was
minimal, Neale's critics suggest, not least because it was English negotiators at
Cateau-Cambrésis who were holding things up in an unsuccessful effort to
secure the return of Calais. If peace abroad was as important for Elizabeth as
Neale claimed, the English negotiators would presumably have tried to speed
things up. The real opposition to Elizabeth came not from the Puritans in the
Commons but from the strong Catholic element in the House of Lords,
especially the Marian bishops who, as Neale himself stressed, presented an
almost united front of opposition to the plans for reformation. This revision
of Neale's thesis tempted the influential revisionist scholar Christopher Haigh
to go even further. He too doubts that Puritan influence was very strong in

1559 and argues that the settlement was made more conservative due to the Catholic element in parliament, whose strength encouraged Elizabeth to follow a more cautious religious policy than most of her advisers wanted.

Whose interpretation is most convincing: Neale's, Jones's or Haigh's? There seems no doubt that Neale over-stated his case and misinterpreted some parliamentary evidence, although some of his conclusions are still consistent even with Jones's description. Haigh probably goes too far in the opposite direction. What we can say is that Elizabeth I was under pressure in 1559 from both sides of the religious divide and that the foreign situation may well have made her cautious and thus delayed the passage of the legislation. It probably also explains why she concealed her true religious opinions from ambassadors: what she told the representatives of Spain and France was, of course, contradictory. What we know of the rest of Elizabeth I's reign suggests that the settlement largely reflected her own views and that she was quite capable of balancing rival factions (a point made, ironically, by Neale in his biography of Elizabeth). Recent revisionist accounts of Elizabeth's parliament, especially those of the great Tudor historian, Sir Geoffrey Elton, suggest that Neale tended to exaggerate the importance of parliament, which would support Jones's thesis against Neale, and probably against Haigh too. Thus, the settlement as reinterpreted by Jones looks less accidental than Neale thought. Elizabeth was a practical politician: she was prepared for a few accidents and had the wit to respond to them positively.

The Act of Supremacy

Henry VIII had made himself supreme head of the Church in England in 1534 and Edward VI had inherited this title. It was the clearest possible rejection of the pope's claims to direct the religious life of the country. If Elizabeth I were to show herself a Protestant, she had to reject papal primacy and re-establish royal control of the Church. Henry and Edward had been 'supreme head' of the Church but, interestingly, Elizabeth took the title 'supreme governor', which has remained the title of all subsequent English rulers, apart from the Catholic James II (1685–88). This change of wording made no difference to the power the queen wielded over her Church, but words are important, especially in titles. It is generally thought that 'governor' represented a less extreme claim to lay control over the Church than 'head', which suggests that Elizabeth was cautiously seeking to please those who might oppose the royal supremacy (or, from a more negative perspective, was bamboozled into it by pressure from devious advisers).

The change of title does not appear to have been part of the initial plans for the settlement drawn up in late 1558, but a later addition made as the legislation was debated in parliament. The suggestion came from Thomas Lever, a veteran Protestant academic and preacher and a returned Marian exile. It may be that the change was made to please Lever's friends, the more forward Protestants, who might have had scruples about calling the queen 'head of the Church' when they recognised in religious matters only the sovereignty of Christ. Christ would be the head and the queen the governor, Christ's lieutenant on earth, or at least in England. 'Governor' in the sixteenth century meant ruler and had been given currency in a famous humanist work of 1531 by Sir Thomas Elyot with the curious title *The Book Named the Governor*.

If Lever was indeed instrumental in the adoption of the new title, then Neale's views would seem at least in part to have been vindicated, since this was a significant change that Elizabeth had not planned. But it has also been suggested that the new title was part of a clever Elizabethan *via media* or 'middle way' policy to placate Catholics, who would be happier with 'governor' than with 'head'. If so, then it would bear out Haigh's views. One scrap of evidence to support this view comes from the Spanish ambassador, who claimed that he had encouraged the queen to accept this new title. However, this may merely have been the ambassador boasting; in any case, if Catholics in parliament preferred the title 'governor' they had a strange way of showing it, since they voted consistently against it in the House of Lords. Nor would they have appreciated the idea that the queen could be second in command to Christ, since they reserved that position for the pope.

One final point to consider is the publication in 1558 of John Knox's wonderfully titled book, *The First Blast of the Trumpet against the Monstrous Regiment of Women*, a piece of male chauvinism written by one of the leading Protestant Marian exiles, a Scot whose career had previously been among the English Protestants. Knox argued that women could not rule men in any capacity, whether as queens or, presumably, as heads of the Church. His book was directed against the three Catholic queens who dominated politics just before Elizabeth I's accession: Mary Tudor; Mary Stuart, queen of Scots; and the latter's mother, Mary of Guise, regent of France. Seldom has an author more seriously mistimed the publication of a book, since within a short time of its appearance, Elizabeth had come to the throne. Knox was one Marian exile who was not welcome to return to England. However, the fact that Lever, a colleague and co-exile with Knox, suggested that the title of head be rejected for a less grand one, and the fact that Elizabeth accepted this, may possibly reflect a desire among the returned exiles not to inflame anti-feminist feelings any further.

Elizabeth I's reign saw a gradual waning of the old Lutheran idea that the clergy should submit to lay authority and the rise of claims, on both the conservative and the radical wings of Protestantism, that they were in some respects exempt from it. It is arguable that by renouncing the headship so easily Elizabeth was making a rod for her own back and for those of her successors, who would be faced with troublesome priests and bishops. But perhaps she felt at this early stage in her reign that she had no choice. Maybe Knox's book was more relevant than is generally claimed.

The Act of Uniformity

The Act of Uniformity of 1559 was also a mixture of the old and the new. Edward VI had passed two Acts of Uniformity, one in 1549 and a second in 1552, which established a uniform liturgy for the whole Church in England, replacing the Latin Mass, which had taken slightly different forms in different parts of the country. The first Edwardian act brought in an English Book of Common Prayer in a translation by Thomas Cranmer, the Archbishop of Canterbury, based on a moderate Protestant interpretation of the Communion service. Cranmer had been anxious to avoid alienating Catholic opinion but in the process had upset more advanced Protestants by the ambiguity of his text: hence the more thoroughgoing Protestant Prayer Book introduced by the second Act. However, in exile under Mary some of the leading English Protestants had moved even further and for them even the second Prayer Book was insufficiently pure in its doctrine. Thus, the Elizabethan regime, once it had accepted the need for an English prayer book, had a choice of possible models and was under pressure from different sides about which to adopt.

The upshot, probably intended from the very beginning, was that the 1552 Prayer Book was adopted with three small amendments; the 1559 Act emphasised that its main purpose was to reinstate the second Edwardian book with these modifications. First, the Act changed the litany (the prayers in the Sunday service asking for God's protection), by omitting the prayer asking for God's protection from the pope and 'all his detestable enormities'. This was a change to both the 1549 and 1552 Prayer Books and is the only part of the Elizabethan settlement that can undeniably be put down to a desire to please Catholics. However, it is difficult to see it as a step to win over English Catholics; rather, it was an attempt to avoid adverse foreign opinion, and perhaps also to prevent Catholics being moved to interrupt the service, a problem to which a part of the Act of Uniformity is devoted. Second, the Elizabethan Prayer Book changed two sentences in the Communion service by amalgamating passages from 1549, which suggested a Catholic belief in the physical presence of Christ's body and blood in the bread and wine, with passages from 1552 that followed the Zwinglian fashion of describing Communion merely as a commemoration of the Last Supper. The words to be used by the clergyman while giving out the bread were as follows:

> The body of our Lord Jesus Christ which was given for thee, preserve thy body and soul into everlasting life; [words taken from the 1549 book] and take and eat this, in remembrance that Christ died for thee, and feed on him in thy heart by faith, with thanksgiving [words taken from the 1552 book].

The wording that accompanied the distribution of the wine followed the same pattern.

The words used in the Prayer Book to explain the Communion service were crucially important and ended up with a very interesting theological compromise. This was once interpreted by historians as an attempt to walk a middle path between the more Catholic wording of 1549 and the reformed formula of 1552, but it has recently been suggested by Diarmaid MacCulloch that the revival of the 1549 wording was probably in order to please a range of Protestant opinion rather than out of a desire to placate Catholics. The old disputes about the Communion between Lutherans, who only partly rejected the Catholic doctrine of transubstantiation, and Zwinglians, who believed in a purely commemorative Communion, had by 1559 to some degree been mediated by the influential views of Calvin, who held that there was a spiritual 'real presence' of God among the people gathered together to partake of Communion. So the hybrid wording of Elizabeth's Prayer Book may not have been as strange as it might at first seem. However, they would have been strange Catholics indeed who could accept the 1559 Book of Common Prayer on the strength of this change to the Communion service, even without the litany against the pope.

The third change involved a technical matter of revising certain of the Sunday readings from the Bible and has excited little controversy among historians.

The Act of Uniformity carried a (moderate) sting in its tail. It concluded by saying that, for the time being, church ornaments including statues, candles, crosses, carvings, wall-paintings and stained glass, and the vestments to be worn by ministers, would be those from the second year of Edward VI's reign, pending a final decision to be made later. What clergymen should wear had been a subject for much learned debate. Catholic priests had seven articles of vesture, all deeply symbolic and richly embroidered, but as, according to Luther, all believers were priests, in Protestant eyes the clergy should not be differentiated so markedly from the laity. There was a surprising degree of agreement among the reformers about this. However, conservative reformers could see the social and political value of having the clergy dressed in a style reminiscent of the Catholic priesthood. There had been serious disputes about this under Edward

VI, and towards the end of his reign, the supporters of less formal attire had come out on top. The question of church decoration was similar, with radical Protestant opinion in favour of destroying all reminders of Catholic idolatry, and conservative Protestants reluctant to oppose decoration and concerned about the social impact of needless destruction. The terms of the 1559 Act of Uniformity make it clear that these disputes were continuing in the early months of Elizabeth I's reign, for the simple reason that it imposed no settlement of them.

Enforcing the settlement

The Elizabethan settlement was enforced on everyone in the country; there was to be no toleration of different religious opinions. This was consistent with views that were widely held in both Catholic and Protestant societies all over Europe. The Act of Supremacy laid down that an oath, by which people swore that they accepted the royal supremacy, be administered to the clergy, to laymen with political or social authority such as judges and mayors, to anyone taking a university degree and to people 'suing livery of lands', that is to say, inheriting freehold property. Those who took the oath accepted that Elizabeth was governor of the Church and rejected papal power. If any office-holder refused the oath, he was to be deprived of his position and disqualified from ever holding office in the future. The Act of Supremacy added that anyone who openly supported the power of the pope, in books or sermons, was subject to a scale of punishments, including imprisonment and forfeiture of property, culminating on the third offence in death. What is remarkable about the initial stage of enforcement of Elizabeth's religious settlement is that she did not use the Act of Supremacy to persecute her theological opponents, as she could easily have done, following precedents set by her father and sister. This seems to have been a conscious policy decision, though it did not meet with the support of all Elizabeth's advisers, especially those who had themselves experienced persecution under Mary.

After the two Acts had been passed, the queen appointed commissioners to enforce the new religious order on the country. They set about administering the oath as their chief mechanism of enforcement. This seems to have been done with a light touch; there was a desire at this stage to avoid conflict and a decision seems to have been made, presumably by the queen and her advisers, for a contrast with the extremism of her sister's reign. There was also a desire to incorporate as many people as possible, both laity and clergy, within the new Church of England.

There had been an understandable decline in the numbers of those seeking a career in the Church in the years before Elizabeth's accession, so there was no desire to lose even more parish priests. It is not clear precisely how many of the roughly 10,000 clergy resigned their jobs rather than turn Protestant, but it would seem to have numbered initially no more than about 5% of the total. This is a highly significant figure in the light of the controversy that has raged among historians in recent years about how Catholic or Protestant the country was in 1559; it may also demonstrate that the commissioners were sometimes prepared to turn a blind eye to Catholic practices.

As the events in parliament in the first few months of 1559 showed, however, Mary's Catholic bishops were more committed to the old ways than were their parish clergy: all the surviving bishops from Mary's reign, except Bishop Kitchin of Llandaff (a rather disreputable figure), refused the oath of supremacy and were deprived of their posts, to be replaced by Protestants. Of 26 such bishops, only 17 were still alive at Elizabeth's accession in any case, largely because Mary had not been able to appoint any new bishops towards the end of her reign because, ironically, she was in dispute with the pope. In addition, Cardinal Reginald Pole, the Archbishop of Canterbury, had died only hours after Mary. What would the new government do to these Marian Catholic ex-bishops? It had the power to make them into martyrs: two bishops were imprisoned in the Tower of London to reduce Catholic opposition in the House of Lords; but once the legislation was passed the policy became softer. The ex-bishops were mostly lodged in a state of semi-imprisonment with their Protestant replacements, and one was even allowed to leave the country.

The Act of Uniformity was also enforced at this stage with the minimum of fuss. The Act forbade the use of prayers and forms of worship not found in the Prayer Book — a warning to both Catholics and more advanced Protestants — under pain of heavy fines: 100 marks (a mark was two-thirds of a pound) or 6 months' imprisonment for the first offence; 400 marks or a year in prison for the second; forfeiture of all goods and imprisonment for life for the third. In effect, any clergyman not using the Prayer Book would be ruined. This was deterrent enough to ensure that this part of the Act seems not to have been used much by the authorities. The Act also imposed a penalty on those who did not come to church 'there to abide orderly and soberly' on Sundays and other holy days, unless they had a good excuse: they were to pay 12 pence for each offence — over a week's average wages — to the church-wardens (lay officials, two in each parish, who helped the clergyman), the money to be given to the poor. This was in line with the Edwardian Act, though the financial penalty was new. The penalty looks minor in comparison with what was to happen later, but it would have deterred most people.

Enforcement at this level was rather slow at first and dependent on the vigilance of clergy and churchwardens and on the support they received from the ecclesiastical authorities. Nevertheless, in 1569 some 180 people were presented to the Archdeacon of Norwich for non-attendance at church and 116 were presented the following year to the Archdeacon of Winchester.

Using her powers under the Act of Supremacy, and following a pattern established in 1536 by Henry VIII and Thomas Cromwell, in the summer of 1559 Elizabeth issued a series of 57 injunctions, detailed orders about how the parish life of the new Church was to be conducted, to be read out in church by the clergyman four times a year. Elizabeth then gave her commissioners the power to conduct a 'visitation' — a parish-by-parish inspection — and to enforce the injunctions. The three most significant aspects of the injunctions commented on by historians were, first, that the clergy were allowed to marry, provided that the wives they chose were 'honest and sober' and that they got the permission of their bishop and two justices of the peace; second, the removal of shrines and images; and third, that the altar was to be replaced by a Communion table, to be placed at the west end of the church when not in use. The use of an altar was associated with the sacrificial element of the Catholic Mass, with Communion in one kind and a belief in relics; a Communion table turned the Eucharist into a Protestant remembrance of the Last Supper. The queen seems to have had to give way on the removal of rood lofts — archways, often beautifully carved, surmounted by a cross (or rood), which separated the chancel from the nave, thus emphasising the importance of the altar. It seems that the queen wished to preserve rood lofts, but was pressurised by her Protestant advisers to agree to their removal. On the vexed question of vestments, the injunctions instructed the clergy to wear 'such seemly habits' as were used at the end of Edward VI's reign, which meant the surplice.

Conclusion: an inconclusive settlement

The settlement of 1559 was the product of a great deal of disagreement, largely between a conservative group of Protestants, led by the queen, and a more forward group, strongly supported by the returned Marian exiles. These disputes over liturgy, ornaments and vestments continued over the next decade and the minutiae of the settlement were endlessly debated for the rest of the reign. In parishes up and down the country similar disputes took place, with a type of underground resistance developing in many areas against the iconoclasm of the injunctions and on the matter of vestments. In Wales, the settlement was not fully applied until 1563, when an Act of Parliament authorised the preparation of a Welsh Prayer Book, though it was not actually published until 1567. However, the really significant change to the settlement was on the matter of enforcement, and this was in response to later developments that could not be foreseen in 1559.

One issue that can be linked both to enforcement and theological controversy was that of the Thirty-Nine Articles. A statement of the main religious beliefs of the new Protestant Church of England had been drawn up in Forty-Two Articles by Cranmer in Edward VI's reign. It might have seemed sensible to do the same in 1559, but whether because the detail of the articles needed changing, or to avoid controversy, the articles were not looked at until a convo-cation, the general assembly of the clergy, met in 1563 and drew up the definitive Thirty-Nine Articles. However, the queen was reluctant to enact them by parliamentary statute, probably because she did not want to see them enforced as a test of belief through the sort of persecution that had been seen under her sister. Finally, however, parliament gave the Thirty-Nine Articles the force of law in 1571, though by then the religious climate had changed consid-erably. It might also be worth remembering that one of the greatest institutional creations of the Elizabethan Church was the Court of High Commission, which was composed both of senior clergymen and of lay politicians and was used to enforce church discipline. It continued into the Stuart period as the most significant administrative link between royal policy and church practice but it was not part of the 1559 settlement: it emerged gradually during Elizabeth's reign, growing out of the initial commissions to enforce the oath of supremacy and conduct visitations to apply the royal injunctions.

Questions

1 How could Neale and Jones reach such different conclusions about the passage of the Elizabethan settlement through parliament if they used the same evidence?

2 If Elizabeth I was the supreme governor of the Church of England with a hierarchy of bishops under her, why did she need to involve parliament in the running of the Church?

3 How fair is it to say that the way in which the Acts of Supremacy and Uniformity were enforced shows the limitations of the power of the Tudor monarchy rather than its strength?

Was there an Elizabethan Puritan movement?

The last chapter looked at the Elizabethan religious settlement of 1559. It was not achieved without opposition from both Catholics and those Protestants who thought that it was too moderate or too conservative. The rest of this book is largely concerned with the continued resistance to Elizabethan religious policy from these two opposite ends of the spectrum, and with how Elizabeth I responded to this opposition. We start with the Puritans.

Were there any Puritans?

Although the word 'Puritan' was coined in Elizabethan times, its use by modern historians has been surrounded by controversy. For modern historians 'Puritan' means a radical or extreme Protestant; indeed, the word has become almost indispensable. It will be used here to describe those Protestants who wished to take the 1559 settlement further, to 'purify' the Church of England of what they saw as its remaining Catholic elements, and who therefore opposed the conservative moderation of the queen. Puritans also tended to support a reformation of manners and a moral climate of high standards in sexual and personal matters, for which they were ridiculed by satirical play-wrights. However, the word did not appear in the English language until 1567, so perhaps it should not be used with reference to Protestant opposition to the settlement of 1559. Moreover, it was generally employed as a term of abuse: most of the people we now call Puritans would not have liked being given this label at the time. The word suggested that they held heretical 'antinomian' views, believing that they were above the law and thus mis-interpreting the biblical passage that said that 'to the pure in heart all things are pure' (Titus 1:15). There was no real agreement among Elizabethans about how to apply the word 'Puritan' and it was not widely used in any case: they tended to use terms like 'precisian' or 'the godly', which the Puritans themselves tended to prefer. Finally, and perhaps most disconcertingly, the word was sometimes used at the time to describe people to whom historians have agreed *not* to apply it. The great chronicler John Stow used the term in 1567 to describe a group of extreme Protestants who would now be seen as separatists, i.e. people who wished to separate themselves from the Church of England. As people who had separated themselves from the Church had given up trying to purify it, historians generally exclude them from the description 'Puritan'. James I published a book in 1603 called *Basilikon Doron* that set out his political ideas and used the word 'Puritan' to apply to extreme separatists like the so-called Family of Love who, again, would not be likely to be called Puritan by modern writers. Historians have spent a great deal of time debating the correct usage of the word 'Puritan' and some use it more sparingly than in the past; nevertheless, it remains indispensable for any study of Elizabethan religion.

Another difficulty with the definition of the word 'Puritan' lies in the different views there were on what needed to be purified in the Church of England, and the range of opinion on how urgently it was needed. It is therefore difficult to speak of a 'Puritan movement' or of 'Puritanism'. If there was a genuine Puritan movement, we would expect a degree of coherence and uniformity in approach; however, it is far from clear that the Protestant opponents of the Elizabethan Church did form a single group, or 'movement', as Patrick Collinson has called it. Geoffrey Elton, in criticising Collinson, even went so far as to describe Puritanism as a 'confusion' rather than a movement, though this is to exaggerate a reasonable point of criticism. There is certainly something in the movement idea, if we are willing to see Puritanism as a loose grouping, a sort of sixteenth-century popular front. Peter Lake used the term 'moderate Puritan' to describe an influential group of academic clergymen who could be found at the heart of the established Church, expressing what would generally be said to be Puritan views. The concept of 'moderate Puritan' may seem difficult to reconcile with the idea of a Puritan movement, but if we see the Puritan movement as a group within the Church of England we understand it best. However, since this movement was contained as part of the Church it is sometimes difficult to say who was a Puritan and who was not, and it may also be difficult to define who was moderate and who was not! Moreover, the Puritan movement changed over the 44 years of Elizabeth's reign, developing new areas of interest and focus, though with a sufficiently strong core of principle and personnel for it to be described as a dynamic movement, if a rather loosely structured one. The rest of this chapter will look at the twists and turns through which the Puritans developed their campaign.

What did the Puritans believe?

From the start of Elizabeth I's reign Protestants were divided between those who were in favour of thorough reform, and those who were content with the moderate changes brought in by the 1559 settlement. This division was as old as the English Reformation: in Henry VIII's reign the battle between conservative and reforming factions was the main theme of the years 1529–47 and it continued in the reign of Edward VI. The Prayer Book of 1549 had been replaced by that of 1552 because of pressure from the more extreme reformers, and Edward VI's reign saw a great dispute over what vestments the clergy should wear. Mary I's accession produced further division: some conformed, some resigned and lived quietly in England, others went into exile. The exiles, many of whom ended up in Frankfurt-am-Main, then split over the question of which Prayer Book to use. The followers of Richard Cox, known as 'Coxians', were content to continue to use the 1552 Prayer Book but the adherents of John Knox, the 'Knoxians', moved on to Calvin's Geneva in order to use a book that was closer to Calvin's own service book, purified of some of the remaining popish elements allegedly to be found in the 1552 one. Exile under Mary brought many English Protestants into direct contact with religious life in south Germany and Switzerland and with the practices and beliefs of the followers of Zwingli and Calvin. In the early years of Elizabeth I's reign, reformers remained strongly influenced by continental practice: leading English Protestants wrote to their old friends in Zurich, nervously seeking advice and reassurance about what they were doing in England. Continental practice also came to England in the shape of Huguenot and Dutch Protestant refugees, who set up their own churches in London, Kent and other places. These churches were allowed to continue to run themselves according to continental, generally Calvinist, models.

The fact was that no one really knew exactly what a reformed church should look like. As the learned men of the English Reformation puzzled out how to reconcile the peculiarities of the English political system with the demands of continental practice and theology, even among reformers abroad there was no absolute theological agreement: well into the second half of the sixteenth century Swiss and German religious beliefs were developing and changing. Calvin was certainly influential on the Elizabethan Church, but his ideas were being refined and extended even on the continent, especially by his successor at Geneva, Theodore Beza. It was hardly surprising that there was disagreement among the 'godly' in England about what direction the reformation should take.

Disagreement centred around four main interrelated points: church government, discipline, the need for a preaching ministry and ceremonies. In terms of the government or structure of the Church, the great — but sole — achievement of the Protestant Reformation had been to abolish papal power and transfer the leadership of the English Church to the monarch. Most Protestants could accept this Erastian transfer of power, given the circumstances in England, but it was hardly ideal when compared with the situation in Geneva and other cities in Germany and Switzerland, where there was a clearer separation of lay and clerical roles and a more significant political role for the clergy. It was considerations of this sort that lay behind the adoption of the title of supreme governor, rather than supreme head, in 1559. If radical Protestants could not accept the leadership of the queen, they had no alternative but to leave the Church altogether, becoming separatists. Very few were willing to do that.

Having reconciled themselves to royal supremacy, however, Puritans found that, in terms of church discipline, almost nothing had changed from the days of the papacy. In Geneva, and among the Calvinist churches elsewhere in Europe, a system of church administration had developed that later became known as 'Presbyterianism'. Under the Presbyterian system, lay elders in each congregation worked with the clergy, who were divided into three ranks: 'pastors' or priests, 'doctors' or teachers, and 'deacons', who took responsibility for charitable work. The running of each congregation was done through a consistory court, where clergy and laity worked together. Representatives of each congregation met at local level in regular meetings called 'classes' (the plural of the Latin word *classis*, a group) and then in regional or national synods. It was most important that under this system there were no bishops: church government in the Calvinist model was democratic rather than aristocratic. However, Elizabeth I's Church retained a 'popish' hierarchy of archbishops, bishops and archdeacons alongside church courts, which still used the medieval canon law of the Catholic Church, though they now dealt, ironically, with the enforcement of the Protestant settlement, as well as with the wills, marriage, sexual matters and defamation that had been their concern for centuries. Cranmer had attempted a reform of the canon law in Edward VI's reign, but there were too many vested interests involved — and too little time — to achieve it. The system of discipline preferred by the more 'godly' reformers with experience of continental practice was rooted in the individual congregation and involved the cooperation of laity and clergy in the setting up of consistory courts. A real Puritan reform in the manners of ordinary people would never be achieved through the creaking Roman system of church courts, but in a 'godly' community, with clergy and laity all pulling together, it might be. The role of local clergymen was crucial, so at the heart of the Puritan plan for a reform of the Church was the production of a preaching ministry of learned individuals, capable of building local communities that could foster discipline and godly living. Moderate Puritans might not wish to create a completely Calvinist disciplinary structure, but they could certainly understand the need to recruit and train learned ministers.

In comparison with these fundamental matters of church government, which presented a real challenge to the unity of Elizabethan Protestantism, the concerns over ceremonies might seem less significant, but they generated a great deal of excitement at the time. Essentially, Puritans wanted the Prayer Book and the injunctions of 1559 substantially modified in order to remove the last vestiges of Catholic ceremonial. Their ideal was a plain service with a minimum of church ornamentation. They had strong objections to 'idolatry', by which they meant the use of religious pictures and statues, and also to the vestments, principally the surplice (a sort of smock or tunic) that clergy were to wear when performing services. The reformers said these garments were a reminder of Catholic vestments. They held that clergy should not be so clearly differentiated from the laity and they objected to the ruling that clergy should wear a distinctive square cap when not in church. The injunctions of 1559 also encouraged the congregation to bow when the name of Jesus was mentioned in the service, a practice that Puritans saw as idolatry, and to use wafers for Communion, whereas Puritans preferred bread, as the 1559 Prayer Book laid down (though, confusingly, this was in contradiction of the 1559 injunctions). Puritans objected to the Catholic practice of springtime Rogationtide processions, when the congregation marched around the boundaries of the parish. The Puritan pamphlet, *An Admonition to the Parliament*, published in 1572 by Thomas Wilcox and John Field, described the Prayer Book of 1559 as 'picked out of the popish dunghill, the mass book' and denounced the continued use of saints' days, the practice of receiving Communion kneeling down, the use of rings at weddings, aspects of the burial service, the use of the sign of the cross in baptism, the practice of midwives christening newborn children if they seemed unlikely to live, and the ceremony of 'churching' women — 'purifying' them in church after childbirth.

Forms of Puritan support and activity

Behind the scenes, Elizabeth I's reign witnessed the development of a strong body of support for the Puritan outlook among the clergy and laity at all levels of English society. It is difficult to disentangle this growing body of opinion from the mainstream of pious Protestants whose attitudes were less radical than those of the Puritans, but there is good evidence for its existence. Puritans received help from Elizabeth I's favourite, Robert Dudley, Earl of Leicester, and his influential relatives; Izaak Walton in the next century described Leicester as 'the reputed cherisher and patron-general' of the Puritans. Other members of the aristocracy were also prominent supporters, including the Earl of Bedford, who had been a Marian exile, and the Earl of Huntingdon, a possible claimant to the throne described by Claire Cross as 'the puritan earl'. Sir Francis Walsingham, the queen's secretary after 1572, was a Puritan sympathiser, as was the treasurer, Sir Walter Mildmay. Among the academics at Cambridge and Oxford were a large number of theologians whose sympathies were with the moderate Puritans, as were those of some of the senior clergy, most notably Archbishop Edmund Grindal.

The gentry and merchants in many areas gave support to Puritan clergy and to those Members of Parliament who continued to press Elizabeth for further religious reform. London remained a centre of support for more advanced religious views, as it had been from the beginning of the reformation period, and the Puritans were strong in certain parts of Essex, Suffolk and the Midlands, where rural industry, especially textiles, brought prosperity, trade and contact with new ideas from abroad. There were even clusters of sympathisers in the towns of the west and the north, where the countryside was more conservative in its outlook. The power to appoint parish clergy often belonged to the local gentry, subject to the formal approval of the bishop, and they could use their rights to see that ministers of a 'godly' outlook were appointed. In many towns the local merchant community took the initiative to appoint clergymen as 'lecturers', who were to some degree outside the control of the Church author- ities and could spread more advanced doctrine through their sermons, whether in cooperation with the local parish clergy or as their rivals. The growth of literacy, the expansion of printing and the reformers' stress on individual piety and religious study contributed to a strengthening of the Puritan outlook among the laity. This was seen, for example, in the faintly comical development in Sussex in the 1580s of the Puritan forenames for children: Sorry-for-Sin, Fear-Not or Sure-Hope replaced the more familiar Thomas, John, Catherine or Anne.

As her reign progressed, it became clear that Elizabeth was unsympathetic to these Puritan objections to the government and ceremonial of her Church and that a growing body of opinion agreed with her. However, the political position was always fluid, and Puritans tried repeatedly to pressurise the queen into modifying the Church. Advocates of further reform used a wide range of methods to get their point across. When one method was blocked they tried another. Methods included agitation in the convocations (assemblies of the clergy, generally held in York and London at the same time as parliament), pressure in parliament, use of the pulpit and the printing press and, eventually, a sort of direct action. We will look now at how these methods of pressure were applied and in the next chapter we will examine Elizabeth I's reaction.

Ceremonies and the vestiarian controversy of 1565–66

The first phase of Puritan activity focused on efforts to remove the popish ceremonial that remained in the Church as a result of the Act of Uniformity of 1559. It was not unreasonable for reformers to expect that they might continue to 'purify' what had been achieved in 1559, just as reform under Elizabeth I's father and brother had been a staged process. When parliament met in 1563 so did the convocations of Canterbury and York, and at the former a moderate list of Puritan ceremonial reforms was put forward. These included abolishing saints' days, an end to signing the baby's head with a cross at baptism, stopping the use of organs in church and giving bishops discretion on whether to allow exceptions to the rule enforcing kneeling at Communion. This last point was intelligent, since levels of support for the old ceremonies varied in different parts of the country, but it was hardly designed to induce uniformity. Although these proposals are often described as 'Puritan' by historians, the petitioners still accepted the use of the surplice. In any case, convocation voted against them, albeit by a majority of one.

In the 1566 parliament six bills were introduced in the Commons in favour of modifications to ceremonial and were blocked by pressure emanating from the queen. The parliament of 1566 was a most difficult one for the queen and this religious quarrel was in large part to blame.

The years 1565–66 did see the question of vestments finally resolved. The Act of Uniformity and the injunctions of 1559 had not in practice settled this difficult matter and the more radical clergy, especially in London, were inclined to break the law and to perform the sacraments without wearing a surplice, which they hated as a symbol of the popish past. Edmund Grindal, Bishop of London, was sympathetic to the views of the more radical clergy in this matter, but the queen and her Archbishop of Canterbury, Matthew Parker, decided in 1565 to enforce a definitive ruling, commanding the clergy to wear the surplice in church and a square cap (a soft hat not unlike the modern academic mortar-board) while off duty. This was made clear, as were other points about clerical attire, in Parker's *Advertisements*, a document issued in 1566 in the name of the queen. This document also repeated the orders about the use of a Communion table and receiving Communion kneeling. These orders were more conservative than the Puritans had hoped for. Grindal was pressurised into enforcing them and he held a meeting of the London clergy at which they were shown a model dressed in the required clothing. As a result of this decision to enforce the official dress code, 37 London clergymen were suspended from their functions by the bishop for refusing to conform, a demonstration both of the strength of feeling on the issue and of the determination of the queen and her supporters to enforce conformity. In the end, most protesters did submit to authority, although the degree of conformity throughout the country in the years that followed depended on the strength of will of the bishops in each diocese and the degree of public support for conformity in each congregation.

Thomas Cartwright and the beginnings of the Presbyterian movement (1571–72)

In 1570 a new and more radical front was opened up by the Puritan critics of the Church of England when the newly appointed professor of divinity at Cambridge, Thomas Cartwright, gave a series of lectures on the Acts of the Apostles, in which he claimed that the early Christian Church described by St Paul was not governed by archbishops, bishops, deans, archdeacons and their church courts, but by a Presbyterian system, based on the free election by congregations of ministers, who would jointly be responsible for discipline. These lectures lost Cartwright his job and he went into exile in Geneva; for the rest of his life he was to be an important figure in the Elizabethan Puritan movement. Cartwright's lectures opened a new Presbyterian campaign that was enthusiastically supported by the leading Puritans. Parliament was due to be called in 1572 and in preparation for it John Field and Thomas Wilcox, who were, with Cartwright, the most prominent Puritans throughout the reign, published a book entitled *An Admonition to Parliament*, in which MPs were admonished or warned to work for further religious reform. This book, and a number of others printed at the same time by other Puritan sympathisers, shocked conservative supporters of the Church of England by the bitterness of the language in which they were written. By adding a demand for Presbyterianism to the request for ceremonial reform, the book represented a significant development in strategy. In the past, most Puritans had found Elizabeth's bishops broadly acceptable as individuals and their office, if not perfect, at least tolerable. In this they had had the support of continental Presbyterian leaders. Theodore Beza, Calvin's successor in Geneva, wrote in 1566 to a supporter in England, commenting on the 'many learned and religious bishops' appointed by Elizabeth. But in 1572 Field and Wilcox described bishops and archbishops as 'drawn out of the pope's shop' and their government of the Church as 'antichristian and devilish and contrary to the scriptures'.

The outspoken language of their propaganda harmed the Puritan cause and the young authors of the *Admonition* were sentenced to a year in prison by the mayor and aldermen of London; nevertheless, their book ran to a third edition in as many months. Presbyterian ideas began to spread, partly because John Whitgift, later Archbishop of Canterbury and already making a name for himself among the conservative conformists, published a book attempting to disprove the teachings of Field and Wilcox, to which Thomas Cartwright then wrote a reply. This battle of the books helped give Presbyterian ideas a wider circulation.

'Prophesyings' and Edmund Grindal (1575–76)

In the mid-1570s the focus of Puritan activity was on the meetings or conferences known by the curious name of prophesyings. These were regular meetings in market towns of the clergy from the neighbouring parishes, who listened to and discussed one another's sermons, sometimes with a lay audience. They were derived from continental reformed practice and were often indistinguishable from other conferences of local clergy, sometimes known as 'exercises', which were arranged by more active bishops and deans. The Puritan clergy in many parts of the country, but especially in the Midlands and East Anglia, strongly supported prophesyings as a way of improving the education and zeal of the clergy. At prophesyings university-educated ministers could help instruct the other clergy whose religious knowledge was deficient — it was a regular Puritan complaint that the religious instruction of the laity was neglected because many of the clergymen lacked the knowledge to educate them. More radical Puritans could see prophesyings as a sort of experiment in developing the local level, or *classis*, of the representative structure associated with Presbyterianism. Equally, prophesyings were encouraged by reforming bishops like Edmund Grindal, who in 1575 was appointed, to almost universal approval, as Archbishop of Canterbury after the death of Matthew Parker.

Grindal's appointment coincided with a substantial increase in the fashion of holding prophesyings, which were beginning to excite concern at the heart of government. Within a few weeks of his appointment the queen commanded Grindal to stop the prophesyings. Elizabeth, supported doubtless by her conservative councillors, was suspicious of the popularity of the exercises among the laity and suspected, probably correctly, that what seemed to some a harmless piece of in-service training and sharing of good practice was actually an effort to undermine the authority of the bishops and hence of the supreme governor of the Church. What is remarkable is that Grindal refused to do what the queen had asked and instead wrote to his bishops drumming up support for the prophesyings. He wrote a foolish letter to the queen in which he compared himself to St Ambrose, the ancient bishop who had opposed the Roman Emperor Theodosius. Elizabeth quickly rid herself of this troublesome priest by suspending him from office and virtually imprisoning him in Lambeth Palace until his death in 1583. Prophesyings were brought, at least publicly, to an end.

The 'classical' movement of the 1580s

As Elizabeth I's reign progressed, Puritan demands for reform of the Church grew stronger and the methods they resorted to became more radical, culminating in the 1580s in the classical movement. Puritan clergymen continued to meet in local groups, especially in their strongholds in the east of England and the Midlands. They avoided the prohibition on prophesyings by excluding the laity, whose attendance had been one of the queen's strongest objections to them. These Puritan meetings, which took place at local, regional and national levels and reached their height in the 1580s, were clearly an attempt to set up a sort of Presbyterian church within the Church of England. The most well known was the *classis* held from 1582 to 1589 in the area around Dedham in Essex, near the border with Suffolk. We know about this *classis* because it kept minutes of its meetings, which were published in 1903 by R. G. Usher. The ministers from Suffolk and Essex who worked together in this group discussed topics that can loosely be described as matters of discipline: the appointment of clergy to their parishes, their conduct once appointed, the observance of the sabbath, morality plays, matters of divorce and illegitimacy.

It would seem that all matters of difficulty and controversy that the members of the group met with in their work were discussed by the *classis*, rather than referred to the dean and bishop of the diocese for advice, as ought to have been the normal practice. In addition, the Dedham clergy corresponded with fellow Puritans in other areas and in London. There seems little doubt that similar meetings were held in other parts of the country, including East Anglia, Warwickshire, London and even Cornwall. From time to time regional and national meetings were held in Cambridge and London, with Field and Wilcox still playing an important coordinating role. It is perhaps an exaggeration to describe these as Presbyterian synods, although they do strengthen the case for an organised Puritan movement.

The 'bill and book' and the Book of Discipline (1584–86)

The 1580s saw the culmination of Puritan agitation and also the beginnings of a concentrated fightback by the forces of Protestant conservatism. The background to this mounting crisis was the domestic and foreign political threat presented to Protestant England by the discovery of Catholic plots involving Mary, Queen of Scots and the development of the invasion plans of Philip II of Spain, culminating in the Spanish Armada of 1588. Meanwhile in Scotland, France and the Netherlands a great struggle (in which the English became involved at various points) was taking place between the forces of Catholicism and of reformed, Calvinist Protestantism. This threatening political and inter-national situation stirred the Puritans in England to more extreme actions, but also weakened their impact, since Puritan opposition to the Church of England could be presented as, at best, mis-timed, and, at worst, disloyal.

The 1584–85 parliament saw a concerted effort by Puritan sympathisers, who used a common parliamentary device of the time by petitioning the queen in parliament to create a learned preaching ministry. In further parliamentary debates sympathisers expressed criticisms of the recent efforts made by the bishops to discipline Puritan clergymen. Late in 1584 Dr Peter Turner MP, a London physician, introduced his 'bill and book' to the House of Commons: the book was the Genevan prayer book, which he wanted to replace the 1559 Prayer Book, and the bill was a proposal to replace bishops with a Presbyterian form of church government. Needless to say, Turner got nowhere with this revolutionary proposal, which was quashed by the dominant Elizabethan loyalists in parliament. The 1586 parliament followed the same course, with an organised campaign of Puritan petitions and the introduction, this time by Anthony Cope, of a fresh 'bill and book', which were as unsuccessful as Turner's had been. By 1585 the London Puritans, strengthened by Cartwright's return from exile, decided to imitate the foreign Calvinist churches by drawing up a 'Book of Discipline', a formal guide to the constitution of their ideal Presbyterian church, covering the work of ministers, congregational rules and regulations and the distribution of power within the various assemblies that made up the church. Walter Travers was probably the chief author of this book, with help from Cartwright and advice from the other leading Puritans. It would have been too dangerous to print the book, which circulated in manuscript, though it was discussed and in some cases subscribed to (formally accepted) by the secretive Puritan conferences in various parts of the country.

This flurry of extreme Puritan activity represents the high-water mark of the movement. After 1585–86, the forces of conservatism, already on the attack since Grindal's suspension, began to score significant successes in a concerted effort to defeat the Puritan programme. This process will be discussed in the next chapter, but before doing so it is necessary to look briefly at the most extreme Protestant critics of the Elizabethan Church of England.

Separatism

What allowed Puritans to survive and strengthen as the reign progressed was their belief that they represented the true Protestant outlook, the true spirit of Elizabeth's Church. They were willing to work for reform within the Church and were strongly opposed to breaking away from it. They were content to 'tarry for the magistrate', to wait for the queen and the more conservative establishment to adopt the programme for reform and purification that they were advocating.

Throughout Elizabeth I's reign, however, a number of Protestants were so radical in their views that they could not accept this policy of waiting. They decided instead to separate themselves from the Church and set up conventicles, secret meetings in which they would worship as they chose without reference to the laws establishing the Church of England. In doing so they were continuing a tradition that went back to the age of the Lollards.

In 1567 a separatist congregation of a hundred 'godly' Londoners meeting in the Plumbers' Hall was discovered by the authorities. Their leaders claimed that they were merely reviving a secret meeting that had its origins in the reign of Queen Mary. The group had been moved to separatism by the suspension of the London Puritan ministers as a result of the vestiarian controversy. Even more dangerous in Elizabethan eyes, both Protestant and Puritan, were the Anabaptists, who believed in adult baptism. Groups of

Anabaptists had met since the reign of Henry VIII and were viewed with particular concern by the authorities; a small number were burnt as heretics by Elizabeth. The Anabaptists had links through Dutch immigrants with continental religious radicalism. The same was true of the Family of Love, a group that followed the mystical teachings of the Dutchman Hendrik Niclaes. 'Familists' were strongest in parts of rural Cambridgeshire, but they also had supporters in the 1580s among Elizabeth's bodyguard. They practised a modified version of separatism, in that they met secretly and distributed highly unorthodox books but also continued their normal religious observances in the Church of England. As a result, and also perhaps because of their friends in high places, by and large they were tolerated.

The failure of the Puritan movement to effect any substantial or immediate change in religious policy in the 1570s and 1580s led to the development of new and much more important versions of separatism. The growth of the classical movement and the attempt in the 1570s and 1580s to set up a Presbyterian church within the established Church of England further encouraged such separatism; what, after all, was the difference between setting up a *classis*, as at Dedham, and creating a separate religious grouping? The Puritans hoped that such congregations would take over the whole Church, linked together by the elaborate Presbyterian structure and by discipline and prayer according to the Genevan pattern. However, in the 1570s and 1580s a number of more extreme Puritans decided in favour of what one of the leading separatists, Robert Browne, called 'reformation without tarrying for any'. Browne, in association with Robert Harrison and later John Greenwood, collected a small group of supporters in East Anglia. Faced with growing opposition to Puritanism in the second half of Elizabeth I's reign, they decided to break away from the Church of England entirely. This led them into an underground existence and in some cases to exile in the Netherlands to avoid the inevitable persecution that such extreme views attracted. This is the origin of what in the next century was called Independency and later became known as Congregationalism. Were such people Puritans? According to the strict modern definition they were not, since they were no longer trying to purify the Church but were prepared to break away from it entirely; but they clearly shared many of the religious beliefs of the non-separatist Puritans, and it seems strange not to use the term 'Puritan' to describe the ancestors of those who in 1620 sailed to America in the *Mayflower* as the Pilgrim Fathers.

When we consider the activities of these extreme Protestants, it becomes clear that Puritanism was a divided movement. The Protestants who wished to modify Elizabethan religious policy varied in the intensity and fervour with which they approached the task; some of them were quite happy to labour at the heart of government and the Church and were content with minor victories; others were impatient and could see no hope of reforming the Church from within. However, this range of opinion and tendency to disagree is altogether typical of movements, and there seems no reason to deny that Puritanism can be described as a movement.

Controversy: parliament, Puritanism and the 'Puritan choir'

How significant was Puritanism and how important was Elizabeth I's parliament? Sir John Neale, writing in the middle years of last century, devoted three important volumes to the history of the parliaments of her reign. He believed, first, that in Elizabeth I's reign parliament became increasingly important and, second, that the development of a committed group of Puritans in parliament was a crucial symptom of this growing importance. Neale was able to fit both these arguments into a broader picture of how English history developed in the Tudor and Stuart periods. He believed that the growth of parliamentary power under Elizabeth I and the development of a powerful Puritan movement began the process that was completed in the 1640s, when in the English Civil War what earlier historians had called a 'Puritan revolution' overthrew the power of the king and replaced it with the pre-eminence of parliament. Neale's studies of Elizabeth I's parliament showed how in almost every parliament of her reign a struggle between the queen and Puritans developed, which was accompanied by a demand in the House of Commons for freedom of speech. One piece of evidence he used was a satirical manuscript from 1566 that contained a list of MPs, accompanied by brief witty descriptions. This, according to Neale, was a 'Puritan choir', an organised opposition group, which in 1559 had forced the queen to adopt a more Protestant settlement of religion than she had originally intended and continued to press for further reforms in subsequent parliaments.

In the 1970s and 1980s, Neale's analysis came under close scrutiny. An American historian, Norman L. Jones, largely succeeded in overturning Neale's interpretation of the settlement as a Puritan victory. Then, in 1982, Geoffrey Elton published a full counter-attack by completely rewriting the history of Elizabeth's early parliaments. Elton tried to show that parliament under Elizabeth was mainly focused on rather mundane matters of law-making and that on the whole it supported the queen's religious policy, as indeed it supported her policy in almost all areas, and did not seek to promote the privileges of parliament at the expense of the prerogatives of the Crown. There was thus no 'high road to civil war' that could be dated back to the 1560s. More specifically, Elton claimed, Neale's so-called 'Puritan choir' did not exist; the satire was a list of MPs with a variety of religious views, some of them closely associated with the royal court. They certainly played no part in derailing the settlement, since the satirical document was written 7 years after 1559, and — as we have seen — the word 'Puritan' was unknown then in any case. Elton's attack on Neale also served to undermine notions that there was a strong or important 'Puritan movement' in Elizabeth I's reign. Patrick Collinson made a robust defence of the significance of his 'Puritan movement' in reply to Elton, but it is fair to say that Elton's view represents orthodoxy nowadays. The whole tone of recent writing on Elizabeth I's religious affairs has also tended to downplay the significance of Puritanism as a subversive force, threatening Elizabeth's religious policy. However, as Collinson pointed out, if Elton had studied the parliaments of the 1580s he might have found it more difficult to characterise the Puritan troublemakers in parliament as insignificant. Perhaps Neale's mistake was to develop the idea of the Puritans as an 'opposition' group. If the Puritans are seen as a group very firmly embedded within the Protestant establishment, as Collinson emphasised, their true importance becomes clear.

Questions

1 Is the term 'Puritan' too vague to be of any use?

2 How applicable were Calvinist forms of church organisation, developed in individual Swiss cities, to a kingdom like England?

3 Why did Elizabeth I think her authority was so threatened by whether or not clergy wore vestments or lay people attended prophesyings?

How successful was Elizabeth I's policy towards Puritans?

If Puritanism is difficult to define, the government's attempts to deal with it are also hard to pin down. The standard account would be as follows: Elizabeth I established a rather weak Protestant Church in 1559, which was unlikely to please her more radical Protestant subjects, who became known as 'Puritans'. Her task was to enforce her religious settlement in order to achieve the uniformity in worship and doctrine that Acts of Parliament specifically called for. The Puritans' aim was to persuade Elizabeth to alter the initial settlement, to force or cajole the queen and parliament into accepting a purer version of Protestantism, closer to the practice of favoured reformed churches in continental Europe. Elizabeth, however, refused to alter what she had settled, causing exasperation among the Puritans and a tendency to turn to more extreme methods. Elizabeth was thus driven to a policy of suppression, which forced Puritans either into a reluctant conformity or into outright separation from the Church, leading to imprisonment, exile and in a few cases death. By the end of her reign, according to this narrative, Elizabeth's policy had in essence succeeded — she had not changed her settlement and the Puritan movement was, to quote Patrick Collinson, 'underground and diverted', dissolved and at an end.

Appeasement

This orthodox view of Elizabeth I's policy towards Puritanism is clearly plausible and we may not wish to depart very far from it; however, it does need to be refined and clarified. First, as we have seen, Puritanism itself changed considerably during the course of Elizabeth I's reign and consisted of different strands and movements. Equally, it is wrong to portray Elizabeth's policy as static; the Church of England defined itself gradually as her reign progressed. What looks, with the benefit of hindsight, like a settlement in 1559 must have felt much more like a tentative experimental step, not just to Puritans but also to the queen and her more conservative allies. For Elizabeth the period of religious settlement lasted at least two decades; it was really only by the later 1570s that the above narrative becomes convincing, both as regards Catholics and Puritans. However, there were profound differences between the Catholic and the Puritan movements in Elizabeth I's reign and therefore major differences in royal policy towards them. Puritans were firmly, and generally confidently, positioned within the Church of England; the 'moderate Puritans' identified by Peter Lake were largely indistinguishable from the 'godly' Protestants who ran the episcopacy and universities. Even the more extreme Puritans like Field and Cartwright enjoyed the patronage of prominent figures in Elizabethan politics and society throughout their lives. Puritanism was unlikely to be 'defeated' in quite the same way that Catholicism might be. The victories of the Elizabethan conservatives over Puritanism were seldom pushed home completely; indeed, it is still a defensible proposition that the Puritans enjoyed a degree of success, especially early in the reign. The 1559 Acts of Uniformity and Supremacy, for example, were arguably more radical than Elizabeth initially proposed; the ruling on vestments in 1566 was not universally enforced, at least outside London, and most of the suspended London ministers were reinstated. The appointment of Edmund Grindal as Archbishop of Canterbury in 1575 was clearly a Puritan victory, made more rather than less clear by his rapid suspension from office (significantly, he was not sacked) the following year. When Whitgift replaced Grindal in 1583 he was constantly baulked in his onslaught on the Puritan clergy by the strength of their support at court.

Elizabeth's policy towards Puritanism and the Puritan response to it has the appearance of a complicated family feud. Elizabeth found herself often having to appease the strong body of Puritan support among her closest advisers and courtiers and making concessions to their sensitivities. Nevertheless, as with her Catholic policy, it is probably best to describe Elizabeth's approach to Puritanism as being divided into two distinct phases: first a period of cautious co-existence, until about 1580, and then a phase of more vigorous suppression for the rest of the reign. These two periods of policy will be discussed in turn before a final assessment of how far Elizabeth succeeded.

Puritanism within the Church of England (1558–80)

The first phase of Elizabethan policy towards Puritanism was one where conservatives and Puritans worked reasonably harmoniously together with a common purpose to make the re-establishment of Protestantism in England a success.

However the process by which the settlement of 1559 was achieved is interpreted, it is plain that a great deal of discussion went on in parliament, the royal court and Privy Council while the measures were being drafted and enacted. The Puritans had to accept much that was not perfect but they were prepared to do so in the hope of further change, encouraged by the fact that the queen and her conservative allies had been prepared to make concessions.

There seems to have been only a half-hearted attempt to enforce a strict line on vestments initially; a considerable degree of diversity was revealed in 1565–66 when the government sought to impose a uniform policy.

One important factor that helped bind the Church together in these early years was the approach adopted by the government in appointing bishops. Mary I had not been able to appoint bishops freely when some of her more elderly prelates died towards the end of her reign, and in 1559 all but one of her surviving bishops refused to subscribe to the royal supremacy. In replacing them, Elizabeth made use of men who were broadly acceptable to Protestants on both wings of the Church. Her Archbishop of Canterbury, Matthew Parker, had not gone into exile under Mary, though in this he was unusual among the new appointments; his approach was generally tolerant and he was respected both by reformers and by more conservative clergy. Many of the other bishops were men who had been in exile and whose outlook was thoroughly reforming: Edmund Grindal, Bishop of London; Thomas Bentham of Coventry and Lichfield; Robert Horne of Winchester; John Jewel of Salisbury; James Pilkington of Durham; Edwin Sandys of Worcester; John Scory of Hereford; Richard Cox of Ely; and William Barlow of Chichester. By and large these bishops shared the Puritan view that the settlement of 1559 was in need of further improvement, but they accepted that it would be a gradual process and that it was wise to allow Elizabeth to follow a more conservative policy for the time being. In 1571 Robert Horne wrote to Heinrich Bullinger in Zurich that 'it would be dangerous to drag her on, against her will, to a point she does not yet choose to come to', though he clearly found this unsatisfactory. One of Horne's chaplains preaching in 1566 claimed that 'the fathers of England [i.e. the new bishops] did not at the first pluck out all abuses, thinking at the length they should loose the root with more ease, and therefore they began with some things and let some others alone.'

The crisis that surrounded the imposition of a uniform rule on vestments in 1565–66 showed a desire on the part of government to adopt a tougher line with nonconformist Puritan clergy; the crisis came because Parker and Grindal were drawn most reluctantly into a showdown with the Puritans. Even after 1566 the degree of conformity to these instructions on vestments and on other matters of ritual and liturgy was probably rather patchy, especially in areas like

Lancashire where it was necessary to maintain the support of the more radical Protestants in the struggle with Catholicism. The promotion of Grindal to Canterbury in succession to Parker meant the appointment of an archbishop who had been unwilling to enforce the vestments so favoured by the queen and who wished to build a Church that was acceptable to all but the most extreme Puritans. Grindal's robust support for prophesyings, and the encouragement he received in this from other senior clergymen, again demonstrates his moderate Puritan credentials.

By the mid-1570s, however, we see contradictory currents at work in Elizabeth's policy towards Puritans. The growing extremism of the 'godly', shown in the *Admonition* controversy, the use of the printing press and parliamentary agitation, combined with the more radical doctrine of Presbyterianism enunciated by Cartwright and Field, served to intimidate moderates and antagonise the queen: hence the suspension of Grindal and the crackdown on prophesyings. However, it was not clear that Elizabeth intended all regular conferences of the clergy to be brought to an end, especially if the laity were excluded from them; the later development of the classical movement showed that this was impossible in any case. The main casualty of this crackdown was Grindal himself; Puritan exercises and clerical conferences carried on, though with less fuss than before.

A harsher policy towards Puritanism (1580–1603)

With the suspension of Grindal and the suppression of prophesyings the atmosphere changed. The new approach was confirmed with the appointment of John Whitgift as Archbishop of Canterbury when the disgraced Grindal finally died in 1583. Whitgift differed from his two immediate predecessors in three significant ways. First, he was an enthusiastic supporter of the ecclesiastical status quo, content to leave the Church as he found it, a conservative Protestant Church with some relics of its medieval past. Second, he was determined to deal firmly with opponents of this conservative religious policy and especially to get it uniformly accepted by the clergy. Third, Whitgift developed a strong relationship with the queen. Alone of Elizabeth's three Archbishops of Canterbury Whitgift was made a privy councillor and enjoyed the distinction of being given a nickname by the queen — he was her 'little black husband'. Elizabeth seems to have liked him in part because, unusually for her bishops, he was unmarried, as her pet name for him emphasised.

Whitgift was helped in his anti-Puritan policy by a growing body of support among the clergy and at court, particularly by Sir Christopher Hatton, the Lord Chancellor. Significant support for a harder line came from Hatton's chaplain, Richard Bancroft, who made it his mission to research the Puritan movement and who collected a great deal of information about its leading figures, which was used when they were eventually brought to trial. His findings were published in books whose titles speak for themselves: *A survey of the pretended holy discipline*; *Dangerous positions and proceedings*.

Whitgift and Hatton did not have things all their own way: there was still a significant body of support among the political establishment for what Bancroft thought were 'dangerous positions'. This was shown by Whitgift's initial effort, begun as soon as he was appointed, to test the loyalty of his clergy by asking them to subscribe to three 'Articles', which he published in the dioceses of his province on 29 October 1583. The first of these Articles concerned the royal supremacy and the third the Thirty-Nine Articles; these were generally quite acceptable to the 'godly' clergy. However, the second article declared that the Book of Common Prayer 'containeth nothing in it contrary to the word of God' and that the subscriber would use it in public prayer and the administration of the sacraments. A great furore, the 'subscription crisis', erupted during the winter and spring of 1583–84, with some 300–400 ministers in the province of Canterbury refusing to subscribe unequivocally to the Articles and being suspended from their jobs. Petitions were sent to London from many parts of the country in support of the suspended ministers, and Puritan sympathisers at court and on the Privy Council were mobilised. In the end a compromise was reached, by which the clergy agreed to a conditional subscription and in most cases Whitgift withdrew the threat of suspension.

Whitgift then changed tack and proceeded against the ringleaders of the Puritans, who had been revealed by the subscription crisis. These ringleaders were subjected to rigorous examination under more detailed articles before the powerful Court of High Commission, the body originally set up to oversee the enforcement of the 1559 settlement but which had developed into a permanent church court. The most objectionable aspect of Whitgift's method of proceeding was that the clergy were put under oath to reply truthfully to the questions they were asked: this was the so-called '*ex officio oath*'. This method of examination seemed to many Puritan sympathisers to deny the principle of English common law that people are innocent until proved guilty.

Again, Whitgift's methods met with strong opposition; late in 1584 the Earl of Leicester, the great ally of the Puritans, presided over a conference at Lambeth in which two prominent Puritans, Walter Travers and Thomas Sparke, debated with Whitgift the merits of the Prayer Book in the presence of other leading politicians and clergymen. This conference was clearly arranged by Puritan supporters to put pressure on Whitgift to back down; Lord Burghley, generally, like Leicester, a supporter of moderate Puritans, had already written to Whitgift describing the *ex officio* proceedings as reminiscent of the Spanish Inquisition. In the face of this influential pro-Puritan lobby, Whitgift had to give way, but he was building up ammunition for victory in the long term. It was clearly a good idea to smoke out ringleaders, as Whitgift had succeeded in doing, and it was sensible for him to back off, in the face of influential opposition, from the suspension of several hundred of the more active and intelligent clergy at one blow. The wisdom of Whitgift's approach was confirmed when his onslaught in 1583–84 provoked a more radical response from the Puritans, especially in parliament, which might alienate their influential but moderate supporters.

In the long term the tide was running in Whitgift's favour. The defeat of the Spanish Armada in 1588 was a significant turning point. First, the war with Spain, which had finally broken out in 1584, made opposition of any sort to the queen's policy seem unpatriotic. Second, as the international situation became safer after 1588, there seemed less reason for the conservatives to refrain from attacking the Puritans, who had been necessary allies in the war with Catholicism. Perhaps the most significant factor was the death in 1589 of Robert Dudley, Earl of Leicester, the foremost defender of Puritanism at court. Other members of the Puritan old guard at court also died: Sir Walter Mildmay in 1589, the Earl of Warwick and Sir Francis Walsingham in 1590. The leading Puritan clergyman John Field had also died back in 1584. Meanwhile, growing Puritan extremism, especially the Presbyterian campaign in and outside parliament in the late 1580s, was alienating moderate support. What was most likely to stir up opposition to Puritans was the way in which the classical movement suggested that they were secretly trying to subvert the structure of the Church of England. The secret publication in 1588–89, at the height of the war with Spain, of a number of scurrilous Puritan pamphlets attacking bishops and the established Church under the pseudonym 'Martin Marprelate' created the impression that the Puritans were dangerous, unpatriotic hotheads.

Against this background Whitgift gained sufficient support to launch a further attack on the Puritan leaders in the autumn of 1589, though, again, it was not as successful as he would have liked: the Puritans still had their supporters in high places. In their search for the secret press where the Martin Marprelate pamphlets were published, Whitgift and Bancroft discovered in the homes of a number of Puritan clergymen in Northamptonshire and Warwickshire a number of documents providing evidence of the establishment in these areas of an embryonic form of Presbyterianism termed by Patrick Collinson the 'classical movement'. As a result nine Puritan ministers, including the veteran campaigner Thomas Cartwright, were arrested, imprisoned and examined first before the High Commissioner (1589–91) and then before the famous Court of Star Chamber. The case against them was that they had sought to undermine the Church and to set up a rival Presbyterian church within a church. Although they could not be executed as a result of a trial in Star Chamber, they could be imprisoned, deprived of their clerical functions and fined. In the event, however, the prosecutions failed: there was still enough high-level support for a tolerant attitude towards this sort of religious dissent.

Late in 1591 Sir Christopher Hatton, the queen's conservative Lord Chancellor, died and the change in climate that resulted meant that by 1592 the case against the Puritan ministers was dropped and they were gradually released from prison. At the same time John Udall, suspected by the government of writing the Martin Marprelate tracts, was arrested and put on trial before the Surrey assizes, after examination by the High Commissioners. In February 1591 he was sentenced to death but then pardoned, following the intervention of King James VI of Scotland (unacknowledged heir to the throne of England), on condition that he leave the country and live in an English merchant settlement on the coast of Africa; in the event he died shortly after he had received his pardon. John Penry, however, another Puritan suspected of involvement in the publication of the Marprelate tracts, was executed in 1593. Whitgift had made his point: the Puritan ringleaders were unable to continue to preach or publish their ideas and were subjected to years of imprisonment and anxiety.

While these criminal cases were proceeding, parliament was also brought to bear on the opponents of the Church of England. In 1593 parliament introduced 'An act to retain the Queen's subjects in obedience', which was directed against 'seditious sectaries and disloyal persons' and which made it illegal to refuse to attend church or to set up separatist congregations, on pain of imprisonment and exile. The traditional reading of this Act sees it as a watershed, an equivalent of the legislation passed against Catholics. It was clearly directed against separatists, and in the same year of 1593 two of the leading Congregationalists of the time, Henry Barrow and John Greenwood, were hanged for sedition. A more sophisticated interpretation might see this legislation as an attempt to bind together moderate, non-separatist, Puritans and mainstream, conservative Protestants in a common hatred of conventiclers. A similar attempt had been made in 1581 when parliament came close to passing an Act against the Family of Love. Perhaps the alleged 'defeat' of

Puritanism in the second half of Elizabeth I's reign was really a decision made by both sides in the conflict to move a little closer together. One way to do this was to turn against common enemies, both Catholics and those on the extreme wing of the Protestant movement.

Puritanism at the end of the reign

Puritans were never again to launch a concerted campaign against Elizabeth I's ecclesiastical policy. Whitgift and Bancroft's onslaught had the effect of silencing the Puritan movement, which had in any case come to something of a halt in the 1590s. However, Elizabeth had not defeated Puritanism. Moderate Puritanism, which formed the bulk of the Elizabethan movement, was deeply embedded in Protestant society, to such an extent that the difference between 'Anglican' Protestants and moderate Puritans is almost impossible to define. What had been created during Elizabeth I's reign, however, was a 'godly', reforming Protestant outlook that would be very difficult to eradicate, despite all of Whitgift and Bancroft's efforts. By the 1590s the Puritan wing of the Elizabethan Church was biding its time, waiting for the queen to die. They put some faith in the emergence of what seemed to be a new protector in the shape of the new royal favourite, Robert Devereux, Earl of Essex, stepson of their old patron, the Earl of Leicester. However, in 1601 Essex led an extraordinary rising, or attempt to seize political power by armed force. He failed, was arrested and was executed for treason, which hardly helped the Puritan cause. Attention was by then focusing on the heir to the throne, James VI of Scotland, who had what turned out to be an unjustified reputation for sympathy with Puritanism.

The death of the queen in 1603 and the accession of James I stirred Puritans into action. James was greeted by the Millenary Petition, which called for the old Puritan reforms long demanded by the movement in Elizabeth I's reign and was signed, as its name suggests, by something like a tenth of the country's clergymen. This strength of support shows that Whitgift had merely succeeded in driving Puritanism underground. James called a conference at Hampton Court to debate Church reform in 1604. However, James took over not only Elizabeth I's realm but also her religious policy and the Puritans met with little success at Hampton Court. Nevertheless, Puritanism survived; indeed it continued to grow and strengthen in the Stuart period. There were profound intellectual contradictions within the Elizabethan Church, which crystallised into the division between 'Anglicans' and 'Puritans'; they were not by any means resolved by 1603 and, according to some interpretations, they led eventually to the great Civil War 40 years later. Whether by accident or design, Elizabeth I's subtle policy towards Puritanism had at least postponed England's wars of religion for a generation.

Questions

1 Was Archbishop Grindal's suspension a sign of the failure of the Elizabethan settlement?

2 Why didn't the Puritans resist Whitgift more vigorously?

3 Did the Puritans have only themselves to blame for their failure?

Did Catholicism survive, revive or decline in the reign of Elizabeth I?

On the last day of Mary I's reign England was a Catholic country; a year later, after the passage of the Acts of Uniformity and Supremacy, England was a Protestant country. This was the effect of the act of state, the decision by the queen in parliament to change the religion of the country. The religious conversion of about three million people, however, could not be effected so rapidly. It could be argued that Elizabeth's task was not as monumental as it might seem: in the 20 years between 1533 and 1553 the country had been cut off from the rest of the Catholic Church and had been open to a gradually increasing level of Protestant influence, both from above and from a growing number of genuine converts to the new religion. The events of Mary I's reign had not been entirely encouraging for Catholicism, especially since the cruelty of her persecution had been counter-productive. Elizabeth might also take some comfort from the fact that there had been no peasants' revolt or aristocratic uprising in opposition to her accession or her religious settlement, and when a Catholic rebellion did break out, in 1569, it was a good example of history repeating itself as farce. On the whole, the parish clergy she inherited from her sister (and brother and father) were willing to accept her settlement.

However, the Protestants did have some problems to resolve. Mary I's reign had seen a revival of Catholicism and the roots of reformation had not gone very deep in a society that was profoundly conservative. The real problem for Protestants was how to move a largely rural, illiterate and tradition-loving society into an acceptance of this highly intellectual new religion. Their best hope was that, with time, Catholicism would simply die out and the new generation would be educated in the new theology. To an extent this is what did happen: Elizabeth was to live a lot longer than the rest of her family, out-living her political and religious enemies. By 1603 it was much easier to claim not only that England was Protestant but also that the English were mainly Protestant, with Catholicism confined to a small minority of the population. The many twists and turns on the way to this outcome will be the subject of this chapter.

Catholicism in disarray: 1559–69

There has been considerable controversy in recent years over how best to describe Elizabethan Catholicism. The most influential view, and probably the most plausible, is that Catholicism in the first 20 years of the reign was going into a steady decline. Elizabeth did not need to persecute Catholics since they were not a serious threat. As with all historical generalisations this view can be attacked on the grounds of dating: there is a strong case for saying that the decline was being halted by 1569, although this did not bear fruit until 10 years later. This description of a declining Catholic community in the early years of the reign was first advanced by Elizabethan Catholic writers themselves, and in recent years has been made popular by Professors A. G. Dickens and John Bossy. According to Dickens and Bossy, the case for a revival of Catholicism under Mary I is far from strong: the bishops she left when she died vigorously opposed the Elizabethan settlement in the House of Lords, but failed to have much impact on it. They showed leadership in resigning, but few of the parish clergy followed their lead and, as a result, the old leaders of the Church were neutralised. There was consequently no active resistance to Protestantism from the Catholic-inclined aristocracy until the revolt of the Northern Earls in 1569.

What counts as Catholicism in the first decade or so of the reign has been described by John Bossy as 'survivalism', the continuation of old beliefs by a dispirited older generation. Little leadership was given to the laity on resistance to the new religion. The obvious step for Catholics to take was to withdraw from Protestant religious ceremonies, either by refusing to take Communion or simply by refusing to go to church. In 1562 at the great Council of Trent the leading Catholic theologians advised English Catholics not to go to Anglican churches, but this advice was not well publicised in England and some of the surviving Catholic clergy advised the laity not to follow it in any case: it would be too dangerous and they would run the risk of persecution. There was a fatalistic feeling among Catholics that they need do little to oppose Elizabeth since, like the rest of her family, she would probably die young. This of course played into Elizabeth's hands — provided she stayed alive! There was little foreign diplomatic support for English Catholicism in the first decade of her reign and, arguably, for its first 25 years. Meanwhile, Protestantism in England steadily strengthened its grip.

Survival and revival

This survivalist inertia was to change in the late 1570s — indeed, the main argument against the 'inertia' theory of Dickens and Bossy is to point out that the seeds of this later revival were already being sown in the 1560s. A large number of Catholic clergy and academics, especially from the University of Oxford, went into exile in the first years of Elizabeth I's reign, settling mainly in the Spanish Netherlands, especially in the university town of Louvain. The Louvainist exiles' main contribution to the development of English Catholicism was to publish in the 1560s about 50 separate religious books, some in Latin but most in English, which were sent to England to sustain the faith of those Catholics who remained at home. They also engaged in controversial battles with Protestant authors, which helped spread Catholic doctrine further: in order to refute Catholic arguments Protestant books, which were freely available, gave readers a reasonably accurate account of what the Catholics were writing. This work was clearly useful, but the Louvainists were at first at a loss to know what else to do: in exile they were unable to influence events in England to any great extent. In this they resembled the Marian Protestant exiles. It was from these early exiles, however, that the Catholic revival was to develop. In 1568 William Allen, former head of St Mary's Hall, Oxford, decided to set up an English College at Douai, then in the Netherlands. This college quickly developed into a seminary, or training college, where young men were to be educated as priests so that they could return to England to work as missionaries.

At about the same time as Allen was laying the foundations for the missionary movement, signs developed of a Catholic political campaign of resistance to the Elizabethan regime, both at home and abroad. Its leading figure was Thomas Morton, a priest who had spent the early years of Elizabeth I's reign in exile in Rome as a member of the ancient English Hospice, a hostel for English pilgrims. This was generally a rather inactive institution, associated with the survivalist mentality of the early years of Elizabeth I's reign, but it was Morton and a number of his colleagues there who launched a movement to persuade the pope to excommunicate Queen Elizabeth and expel her from the Church, calling on her subjects to rebel against her and on Catholic rulers in Europe to depose her. Pope Pius V finally issued his bull of excommunication in 1570, nearly 12 years after Elizabeth's accession; it was the first clear sign that the Catholic Church was going on the offensive. It was, of course, unlikely that life for Catholics in England would be improved by the publication of the bull, since it would be likely to lead to persecution, but it certainly signalled an end to a period of drift.

Morton hoped that the publication of the bull would stir up a Catholic rebellion in England, supported by Philip II of Spain in some sort of military campaign. Philip was a devout Catholic with imperialist ambitions; he had of course been king of England, as husband to Queen Mary. Moreover, the bulk of the English Catholic exiles lived in his territory, the Spanish Netherlands, where Allen was already beginning to develop the missionary movement. Morton travelled secretly to England early in 1569 to stir up rebellion, especially in his native Yorkshire. However, it proved impossible for him to arrange for the excommunication of Elizabeth in Rome and the rebellion in England to take place together, when they would have had more likelihood of success. The papal authorities were remarkably reluctant to act, partly because Spanish diplomacy was protecting Elizabeth. Philip II was much more worried about France than England, and did not wish to jeopardise Elizabeth's neutrality. In the event, all that happened was an unsuccessful rebellion in the north of England late in 1569, the 'Rising of the Northern Earls', led by two military and political lightweights, the Earls of Northumberland and Westmorland, neither of whom was actually a strongly committed Catholic. The rebels did briefly take over Durham and the Catholic Mass was said again in the cathedral there, but the rising was quickly suppressed. It was poorly supported, poorly led, and badly mistimed; nevertheless, it was the first occasion, in over 10 years, when there was any real Catholic resistance to Elizabeth. The flurry of political, diplomatic and religious activity in the years 1569–70 died down. Elizabeth was, if anything, even more secure and the Catholic revival subsided. Moreover, Elizabeth still resisted calls to persecute Catholics on a large scale: she would still try and out-live her opponents.

The seminary movement and the Society of Jesus

Those historians who saw the early years of Elizabethan Catholicism as a period of decline or 'survivalism' point to the second half of the reign as a time of renewed Catholic vigour. However, this revival grew out of the work of Louvainists and exiles like Morton and Allen in the earlier period. In 1568, at the suggestion of a Dutchman, Jean Vendeville, Allen founded the English College at Douai, where he was already a university teacher. Initially he probably did not intend it to be any more than a college of the university, where English students could live and study. However, after the failure of the Rising of the Northern Earls and the badly timed publication of the bull of excommunication the following year, Allen decided to use the college as a seminary to prepare English priests to return to England as missionaries. The setbacks of 1569–70 had shown that Protestantism was not to be overturned quickly; a different course was needed. Allen presumably drew inspiration from the Catholic missionary movement in Asia and America; his work was certainly consistent with the ideals of that nebulous movement known as the Counter-Reformation. The Counter-Reformation (the term was coined at the time) was two things at once: first it was a broad campaign to win back souls lost to the advancing tide of Protestantism; second, it was a Catholic Reformation, a movement to purify the corruptions of the Catholic Church and develop a religion better suited to the more rational and less superstitious world the humanists had created. If we can successfully identify Allen and his movement as agents of this Catholic Reformation, then the arguments of Dickens and Bossy — that medieval English Catholicism was dying in the 1560s and required a new force to revive it — are vindicated. This does indeed seem an acceptable account. What Allen did was new and had an important impact: his was not a movement to preserve the quaint, rustic practices that historians like Scarisbrick and Duffy have so painstakingly described from their Victorian sources. The seminary priests' message was spiritual and theological, not folkloric.

Allen's foundation at Douai was forced by civil war in the Netherlands to remove to Rheims in France in 1578 and was then forced back again in 1593 by the French Wars of Religion. Despite this it had grown into a major establishment by the end of Elizabeth I's reign. The decaying English Hospice in Rome was refounded in 1579 as a second training college and Robert Persons, Allen's chief lieutenant, founded two colleges in Spain, at Valladolid and Seville. The first seminary priests from these colleges arrived in England in 1574 and the number steadily increased as the reign progressed. It is thought that about 800 Catholic priests had been trained in these colleges by the end of Elizabeth I's reign; of these, roughly 180 did not return to England at all, and a further 140 do not seem to have worked there in Elizabeth I's reign. Only 471 are definitely known to have worked in Elizabethan England. They were spread very thin on the ground: the experts in the field, Patrick McGrath and Joy Rowe, calculate that in any one year in the last two decades of Elizabeth's reign a maximum of 150, and at times as few as 100, were at work in England. That number is about 1% of the Protestant clergymen. Nevertheless, to set up a system able to train, transport, lodge and find placements for such a number of missionaries in the face of the vigilance of the Elizabethan authorities, who had armed themselves with a terrifying array of legal weapons, was a tremendous and unprecedented achievement.

The life of these priests was very dangerous because Allen's decision to send missionaries to England inspired Elizabeth to change her policy to one of persecution (which will be discussed in the next chapter). Of the 471 seminary priests who worked in England, 292 (62%) are known to have been captured by the authorities; 120 seminary priests and a further three Catholic priests ordained in England before 1559 were executed; others were imprisoned for long periods, and some were deported. Priests needed to live more or less on the run: in manor houses up and down the country 'priest's holes' can still be seen behind fireplaces or concealed by false ceilings and walls, where the missionary priests hid from the pursuivants, government officials sent to hunt them down. There was even a specialist Catholic builder, Nicholas Owen, who travelled the country constructing these hiding places. The priests were trained in the seminaries to conceal their identity and were allowed to use equivocation if directly questioned by people intent on their arrest. Equivocation meant giving ambiguous or evasive answers and even, in extreme cases, lying.

The Catholic Reformation also came to England in the second half of Elizabeth I's reign in the shape of the Society of Jesus. This famous order of priests, founded in 1540 by the Spaniard Ignatius Loyola, had the express purpose of counteracting, through teaching, study and pastoral work, the effects of the Protestant Reformation. It soon gained a reputation for the calibre of its members, known as Jesuits, and for efficiency. In the 1570s it began to attract English recruits, including two brilliant Oxford Protestants, Edmund Campion and Robert Persons, who abandoned their academic careers, converted to Catholicism and went abroad to train as missionaries. In 1579 the Society of Jesus took over the management of the English College at Rome; it was also responsible for running the two Spanish seminaries and a school founded by Persons in Eu in Normandy, where boys were prepared for higher education in the colleges. In 1580 Persons, Campion and a group of about a dozen other seminarists, some Jesuits and some secular priests, set out for England to lead a well-publicised missionary effort. They even brought with them the surviving Catholic bishop from Mary I's reign, Thomas Goldwell, who had been living in exile in Rome, though Goldwell was old and infirm and in the end did not cross the Channel with the others. The number of Jesuits who worked as missionaries in England was always small, but the impact made by the involvement of the Society in English Catholicism was immense.

Robert Persons worked closely with Allen and after Allen's death in 1594 became the foremost English Catholic, deeply involved in the management of the seminaries and the mission. Persons was a great writer of religious and political books, both in Latin and English; a significant aspect of the Elizabethan Catholic movement was its publication of a large number of books. These were mostly printed in the Spanish Netherlands or France and then smuggled back to England for distribution there. The Catholic Church had learnt from its enemies to use the printing press and the vernacular as Counter-Reformation weapons to propagandise the faith. These books reflected the new Counter-Reformation Catholicism rather than Chaucerian folk religion. Persons' best-selling book was the *Christian Directory*, first published in 1582 and reprinted frequently. It consisted of a simple, straightforward description of the beliefs of a Catholic Christian. Soon after its publication an enterprising Protestant clergyman called Edmund Bunney adopted it, not surprisingly without acknowledgement, as his own work and republished it as a statement of Protestant beliefs. He needed to make few changes to the text: the faith of the Jesuit was not remarkably different from that of the entrepreneurial Protestant. 'Bunney's book' also sold very well and in the seventeenth century it was instrumental in the conversion of Richard Baxter, who became a prominent Puritan. Among the books published by the Catholics was a new English translation of the Bible. In 1582 the New Testament appeared in a translation by Gregory Martin at the Douai/Rheims seminary with a great array of Catholic footnotes and the next reign saw a Catholic translation of the Old Testament. The use of the vernacular scriptures, directed clearly at the literate laity, had also been adopted by the Elizabethan Counter-Reformers from the armoury of the Protestants.

The impact of the seminarists

What was the impact of this revived Catholicism on England? Christopher Haigh has downplayed its achievement. He was keen to challenge the views of Bossy and Dickens and to show that there was not a huge difference between the early efforts of the survivors from Mary I's reign and those of the famous seminary priests. Using evidence from his research into Lancashire, the great 'sink of popery', Haigh showed that a Catholic revival had already started in Mary's reign. Dickens's studies in Yorkshire suggested the reverse. Haigh concluded that the impact of the seminarists was less significant than Dickens supposed. Bossy tended to exaggerate the differences between early Elizabethan Catholicism and the work of the later seminarists and Jesuits. It is also clear that Catholicism was in a more parlous state by 1603 than it had been in 1558: 40 years of Protestantism had taken their toll. Bossy's calculations, based on a survey taken at the beginning of James I's reign, suggest that there were perhaps 40,000 committed Catholics in the country, out of a total population of about 4 million. This proportion might look too small to be significant, but the Catholic revival of Elizabeth I's reign had prevented the complete eradication of the Catholic population in England. Catholics were strong in certain pockets around the country, especially in Lancashire but also in Yorkshire, Staffordshire and Wales and, in smaller numbers, in odd corners of Norfolk, Herefordshire and Sussex. Catholicism had a disproportionate level of support among the gentry in these areas: a skeleton service of something over one hundred active seminary priests could not make much impact on the population as a whole, but it could sustain the old religion among those whose wealth and social standing made it difficult for the authorities to confront them.

About half of the seminary priests came from the gentry; when they returned to England they naturally sought refuge among their friends and relations in this class. Haigh has criticised them for this, alleging in effect that they did not make enough use of the opportunities they had to convert people across the full social range. He has also attacked many of the seminarists for not working in the north of England, where, he claims, there was more chance of success than in the south. This criticism, which somewhat contradicts the first, is hardly fair. It seems unlikely that Haigh is in a better position 400 years later to advise seminary priests on how best to operate than they were themselves. Had they left the comfort of their lodgings among the gentry they would have been captured by the government.

An important aspect of the survival of Catholicism was the ideology of struggle and martyrdom, which the hunted priests clearly exemplified. For the laity the most open act of defiance was recusancy — refusing to obey the laws laid down in the Elizabethan settlement, especially the Act of Uniformity, which demanded attendance at church. The seminarists took a harder line on this matter than most of the old Marian survivalist priests had, with the result that after about 1580 a large number of the Catholic laity attempted to affirm their faith by staying at home on Sunday morning. The government met this behaviour with an increase in the penalties for recusancy. However, the Elizabethan Counter-Reformation was nothing if not flexible. Just as the seminary priests were taught to avoid putting their lives in danger, so they permitted the practice of occasional conformity — attending church sufficiently often to avoid prosecution — though they still advised the laity to resist as much as was within their power. If Catholicism survived in England while in other parts of Protestant Europe it died out, it did so because of the seminarists.

Treason and plot

Was this Catholic endurance what William Allen and Robert Persons wanted? The answer must be yes and no. On the one hand, Catholicism's survival vindicated the decision to preserve the community in England through missionary activity, which was taken after Elizabeth I's first decade as monarch had shown that something more than writing books in exile was needed. On the other hand, Persons and Allen intended the survival of a community of Catholics in England to be a means to a more ambitious end, namely the conversion of the whole country. There were two theories about how this would be achieved. The first was a providentialist, quietist one: that God would not abandon England to heresy forever and that the accession of a Catholic would eventually produce another act of state that would enable the underground Catholic community to come into its kingdom at last. The second theory was more political: that it was the task of Catholics to plot with the enemies of Elizabeth to overthrow Protestantism and re-establish the Catholic Church. There is little doubt that some Elizabethan Catholics over the years supported this second line of action. They were given full papal support by the bull *Regnans in Excelsis* of 1570, in which Pius V not only declared Elizabeth excommunicated but also called on Catholics to depose her.

There were two main periods when a successful Catholic uprising might have happened. The first was the late 1560s and early 1570s, when Mary, Queen of Scots, the Catholic heir to the English throne, arrived in England only to be imprisoned by Elizabeth I, and when Philip II of Spain began to face down his Dutch Protestant rebels. The result was the 1569 Rising of the Northern Earls and the subsequent Ridolfi Plot (1570–71), both attempts to release Mary and to prepare the way for military support to be sent from Spain. Both plots failed quite pathetically. The next phase came about 10 years later, coming to a head in 1588, when the Spanish Armada sailed for England, and carrying on until the end of the reign. This threat, which consisted of some rather unconvincing plots in the 1580s and a far from unconvincing Spanish invasion attempt, proved a failure but it dominated almost all aspects of English life for the last 25 years of the reign.

How far were Elizabethan Catholics implicated in these attempts to overthrow the queen? This has been a matter of great controversy. It is certain that the exiled Catholic leaders of the mission, above all William Allen and Robert Persons, were at times deeply involved. They published works of political philosophy supporting the theory of 'papal power in temporals' — the idea that the pope had the authority to depose a heretical ruler — and they plotted as best they could to involve foreign rulers and domestic conspirators in the attack on Elizabethan England. However, the Catholic laity at home and the missionary priests hiding in the manor houses of the gentry were in no position to do anything but watch from the sidelines. Moreover, exiles and Catholics at home were all in a great dilemma over whether to get involved in political matters. Outright political resistance was supported by the papal bull of excommunication and seemed to be the more glorious path to follow, but there was no point in adopting this policy unless it was likely to succeed; for most of the reign it was far safer for Catholics to make a clear separation between their religious opposition to the Church of England and their continued loyalty to the queen.

The divisions within the Catholic movement at the end of Elizabeth I's reign

Even setting aside the division into survivalists and revivalists, which later historians have sought to impose on Elizabethan Catholics, there were very real disagreements among Catholics throughout the reign. Unlike the debates between different factions of Protestants, these Catholic divisions did not involve matters of theology: all Elizabethan Catholics shared the same set of beliefs. The major disagreements were about how far to take resistance to the Elizabethan regime.

Resistance could take two forms: religious and political. On religious resistance, there was constant disagreement between those who favoured recusancy and those who were less convinced. The official Catholic line was to refuse to go to Protestant church services, but all leading Catholics accepted that the laity could not be expected to follow this brave path in the face of persecution and that they could instead practise occasional conformity.

On political opposition there was less agreement. Until the early 1580s Catholic policy was almost always unequivocal: Catholics might plead with the queen for her mercy but they would not support armed resistance to her government. They were trying to portray Catholicism as a respectable, law-abiding religion, in contrast to the rebelliousness of Protestants. In the dangerous years 1568–72 — when Mary, Queen of Scots came to England, the pope issued his bull and the Northern Earls rose — leading Catholics such as Nicholas Sanders and Nicholas Morton took a more robust line. They argued in favour of deposing the queen, but this approach was never strongly supported, at least not openly, and after 1572 the leading Catholics returned to passive obedience, accepting Protestant government and praying for toleration. This approach was consistent with the policy adopted by Allen of sending missionary priests to England; they were told to instruct English Catholics to accept Protestant political authority rather than resist it. So in 1580 when Persons' and Campion's famous mission left for England they secured from the pope a 'rescript' or revision of the bull of excommunication, in which Catholics were told that they did not need to obey the bull 'as things stand at the moment'. However, as relations between Spain and England deteriorated, leading to open warfare from 1584, the teaching of William Allen and Robert Persons changed, and for the next 10 years or so Catholic books that encouraged rebellion and a Catholic invasion of England were printed. This was a sensible course to take, provided the rebellion or invasion worked; if they failed (and they did), such an approach could only add to the dangers the Elizabethan Catholic community faced. This dilemma led to a clash between those in favour of political resistance and those in favour of a return to passive obedience.

By the end of the reign, almost all the Catholics had returned to political passivity. Of course, the greatest of all Catholic plots occurred in 1605 when Thomas Catesby, Guy Fawkes and friends planned to blow up the new king, James I, along with both houses of parliament, but this was the exasperated response of a tiny minority of Catholics to the new king's failure to grant them a wider measure of toleration. Catholics, like Puritans, pinned great hopes on the new king; all were disappointed.

The debate among Elizabethan Catholics over political policy, whether to resist authority or to compromise, left scars. Disagreements over strategy were added to by the stress caused by exile, persecution, imprisonment, failure and struggle, and were also made worse by clashes of personality and style. The Jesuits, led by Persons, inspired admiration but also jealousy, and in the years 1598–1603 a movement developed among an influential section of the secular priests, with support from some of the Catholic laity, to reduce Jesuit influence over the English mission, especially in the government of the seminary at Rome. In 1598 George Blackwell was appointed by the pope as archpriest, or superior, to the English mission. There had long been a need for such a figure, not least because the sacrament of confirmation could not be performed by the missionary priests; Blackwell was given this authority as if he were a bishop. However, the secular priests rejected Blackwell's appointment because they suspected him, with reason, of being pro-Jesuit. These secular priests appealed to Rome (with the disingenuous support of Elizabeth I's government) to have Jesuit power in English Catholic affairs reduced and to have Blackwell dismissed.

This group, who made two appeals to Rome, became known as the Appellants. At the same time a number of bitter pamphlets were printed by both sides in the archpriest controversy. English Catholics were now using the printing press against each other rather than against Protestants. The Appellants were vigorously opposed by Robert Persons and the Jesuits, who had the real influence over papal policy in Rome, with the result that the Appellants were imprisoned when they got to Rome to present their appeal; by the end of the reign they had met with little success.

This archpriest controversy, or the affair of the Appellants, might look like a storm in a teacup, but it divided the Catholic community along lines that were to continue well into the future. Above all it showed that Catholicism by 1603 was in difficulties: politically defeated, ground down by the gradual growth of Protestantism and divided into rival camps. But it was still there. A small number of Catholics persisted in some areas of the country and a rich tradition of exile, literature, struggle and spirituality was being created. By 1603 Catholicism had become the first substantial English nonconformist sect. It had survived.

Documentary analysis: Catholic attendance at Protestant churches

Case 25: Is it lawful for Catholics who are reconciled to the Church to go on any pretext to the churches or sermons of heretics: for example, may servants, underlings, or sons accompany their masters or fathers to church if they are determined not to pay attention to what the heretics say there?

Resolution. I reply that, as has been said above, it is lawful by natural law, to go occasionally in the circumstances laid down in the nineteenth and twentieth cases of the second chapter.

Solution of Allen and Persons. They refer themselves to the following cases.

Source: Holmes, P. J. (ed.) (1981) *Elizabethan Casuistry*, Catholic Record Society, p. 120.

This rather brief, dry, technical document is an extract from what was probably used as a training manual in the early 1580s in the seminary for English Catholic priests in Rome. A number of questions were posed for an unnamed teacher to 'resolve'. These were questions of the sort likely to be faced by seminary priests returning to England. They were then referred to William Allen and Robert Persons, the two leading English Catholic clergymen in exile, who added their own 'solution'.

We can be reasonably certain that the seminary priests would adopt the approach they were taught when it came to giving advice to the laity. The case here asks whether Catholics in England may practise 'occasional conformity' — in other words, whether they may go to the Protestant churches — at a time when 'recusancy' or the refusal to go to church could lead to severe punishments from Elizabeth's government. The answer given is that they may, and the reason provided is that 'natural law' gives them the right to do so: in other words, they may go to church on the grounds of self-protection, to avoid suffering the harm that they risked if they practised recusancy. The case envisages a rather limited circumstance in which attendance at a Protestant church service might take place, and is not a general permission to avoid recusancy. It is set in a context of other cases (referred to in the 'resolution' and 'solution'), which try to help the Catholic laity avoid the dangers associated with attempting to separate themselves from Protestant society.

The significance of the document is that it shows that occasional conformity was tolerated by Allen and Persons, and presumably by the seminary priests. Hence it is difficult to argue, as Bossy and Haigh have done (from different perspectives), that there was a great difference between the 'survivalists' and the 'revivalists' of Elizabethan Catholicism. It also makes it difficult to define 'Church papists' as a group distinct from the recusants, and tends to make the term 'occasional conformists' a better one. It helps explain how Elizabeth's policy of persecution had the impact of grinding down active resistance to the Protestant settlement, but it also supports the view that in 1603 the almost universal attendance of the English at church represented a wholehearted acceptance of Protestantism.

Questions

1 Was it a mistake for English Catholics to go abroad?
2 How useful were the Jesuits to Elizabeth I?
3 Was it in the interests of the English Catholic community for the Appellants to fail?

Was Elizabeth I's policy towards Catholics consistent?

Elizabeth I's Catholic policy underwent a major change halfway through her reign and it represented the most radical modification of her settlement of 1559. Her attitude towards Roman Catholics became harsher as the reign progressed, changing from a form of toleration into outright persecution. In this respect her policy towards Catholics mirrored that adopted towards Puritans, but it is worth emphasising that there was a huge gulf between the way in which Elizabeth approached Puritans and how she treated Catholics. Indeed, it is arguable that the strengthening of the laws against Catholics was partly in response to Puritan pressure and also from a desire to reunite the queen's Protestant supporters against a common enemy.

The considerations behind Elizabeth I's policy towards Catholics

The considerations that the queen and her councillors had to bear in mind in formulating this policy towards Catholics were complex. Probably least significant in Elizabeth's mind, though perhaps more important in the eyes of some of her advisers, were theological concerns. Elizabeth's policy was not geared to eradicating some heresy or false belief; she was interested purely in maintaining political stability at home and abroad.

In foreign policy, Elizabeth tried to maintain reasonable relations with her powerful Catholic neighbours. It is worth emphasising just how powerful these countries were. Protestantism had little support in Europe; Dutch, Scottish and French Protestants looked to Elizabeth for aid, not vice versa. If Elizabeth wanted peace it made sense not to antagonise the most powerful monarch in Europe, Philip II, ruler of Spain, ruler of the Spanish colonies in the New World and the

Pacific and, just across the Channel, ruler of the Netherlands. He was also Elizabeth's brother-in-law. Philip was a committed Catholic who soon found himself engaged in a sort of crusade against a Protestant revolt in his possessions in the Netherlands. France, with whom England was at war at the beginning of Elizabeth I's reign, was a Catholic country and England's ancient enemy; Elizabeth tried to neutralise it by the simple method of offering to marry one of its princes. This policy of pursuing peace by balancing the two great Catholic powers, Spain and France, would not be helped by an anti-Catholic policy at home. However, in the 1580s such concerns began to disappear as France descended into full-scale religious civil war and Philip II decided that he had to fight England if he was to defeat the rebels in the Netherlands. Thus the change in English foreign policy in the 1580s coincided with a change in policy towards Catholics.

Nevertheless, domestic concerns were probably more important than these foreign worries in developing religious policy. Elizabeth seems to have wanted to emphasise the differences between her government and that of her sister, Mary. Persecution of Protestants had been the hallmark of Mary I's reign, with some 300 burnt at the stake. Such persecution was repulsive and unpopular and Elizabeth tried to avoid it. Martyrological literature of the time stresses the cruelty involved in religious persecution; Foxe's *Book of Martyrs* was embellished with graphic woodcut illustrations of torture, and anyone who reads Tudor literature can see that people at the time were as sensitive to suffering as we are. However, it seems unlikely that this was Elizabeth's main reason for avoiding persecution: public execution was standard practice, the death penalty was frequently resorted to, even for minor thefts, and gruesome methods of execution were not uncommon. In any case, during Elizabeth I's reign a small number of extreme Protestants were burnt at the stake. The real argument against religious persecution was not that it was cruel or inhumane, but that it was ineffective and counter-productive. The early church father, Tertullian, writing in the fourth century, put his finger on the problem: 'the blood of the martyrs is the seed of the Church'. People's faith is strengthened rather than weakened by seeing their fellow-believers killed for their beliefs. Far from rooting out unorthodox ideas, persecution often spreads them. Hence, Elizabeth's gentle policy was a deliberate act of state: Catholicism was to be ignored, rather than advertised by show trials and staged executions.

This Elizabethan policy of moderation was described in a celebrated passage by Francis Bacon:

Her Majesty, not liking to make windows into men's hearts and secret thoughts, except the abundance of them did overflow into overt and express acts and affirmations tempered her law so, as it restraineth only manifest disobedience in impugning and impeaching advisedly and maliciously her Majesty's supreme power, and maintaining and extolling a foreign jurisdiction.

Bacon's description was a clear statement of what was accepted in the first half of the reign as royal policy. In 1570 Francis Bacon's father, Nicholas, Lord Keeper of the Seal and a prominent Elizabethan politician, was commanded by the queen to make the following announcement in the Star Chamber, which was clearly intended to reach a wide national audience:

Her Majesty would have all her loving subjects to understand that as long as they shall openly continue in the observation of her laws and shall not wilfully and manifestly break them by their open acts, her Majesty's meaning is not to have any of them molested by any inquisition or examination of their consciences in causes of religion.

This statement dates from 12 years after Elizabeth I's accession: the policy of mildness was not simply adopted to help the new regime survive the difficult first months of transition from Catholicism to Protestantism. Moreover, the Lord Keeper's affirmation of a policy of not making windows into people's hearts was made after the Elizabethan regime had come through the crises of 1568–70, a period that might easily have provoked government to adopt a tougher line. This was made clear when Nicholas Bacon added that the queen was 'very loth to be provoked by the overmuch boldness and wilfulness of her subjects to alter her natural clemency into a princely severity'.

Elizabeth's approach to the 'old religion' has to be set against the background of her desire to make her regime an inclusive one. At court and in the council there were always people whose attitude to religion can best be described as 'crypto-Catholic' and others who were by no means supporters of the 'godlier' councillors. The Duke of Norfolk, a lukewarm, conformist Protestant from a family of religious conservatives, was a prominent figure at court in the early years, and the Catholic Earls of Northumberland and Westmorland were also intermittent courtiers before their 1569 rising. Throughout most of the reign Sir Christopher Hatton, as courtier, councillor and Lord Chancellor, was inclined to favour Catholics, even in the difficult years towards the end of the reign. Elizabeth's own views were hardly Puritan and showed at times a fondness for old forms of worship. In her Chapel Royal Elizabeth patronised two great musicians, Thomas Tallis and William Byrd, both of them exceptionally gifted composers and both of them Catholics who adapted their compositions to suit a Protestant liturgy, while still carrying on the traditions of Catholic church music. Byrd met the Jesuit missionary priest, William Weston, in 1586 and his family were regularly under investigation for recusancy but were protected by Elizabeth.

Early policy towards Catholics, 1558–80

It is too much to claim that Elizabeth I's policy towards Catholics in her early years was one of toleration. Toleration means permitting a number of different, and sometimes opposed, religious beliefs and practices; this was simply not an option for any English government at that time. In the words of the queen's secretary, Sir William Cecil, 'the state could never be in safety where there was toleration of two religions, for there is no enmity so great as that for religion, and they that differ in the service of God can never agree in the service of their country'. The 1559 Act of Supremacy threatened severe punishment (though not death) for refusing the oath of supremacy; the Act of Uniformity introduced harsh fines, loss of employment and imprisonment for those clergy who used a different Prayer Book from that laid down in the Act. In 1563 the penalties for refusing the oath were made more severe, including death for a second offence, and the number of people who could be forced to take it was extended. Nevertheless, although the oath of supremacy was used in 1559 as a test of men's 'secret thoughts' and did lead to almost all the bishops losing their positions, the enforcement of the settlement was generally conducted in such a way as to avoid pushing people into attacking it or generating a crusading spirit among the more fervent Protestants.

The best example of this early leniency is the treatment of the Marian former Bishop of London, Edmund Bonner, who escaped execution despite his second refusal of the oath of supremacy (unlike another high-profile Catholic, Sir Thomas More, who was executed in Henry VIII's reign for a similar repeat offence). Following the passage of the Act of 1563 increasing the penalties for refusing the oath of supremacy, the queen seems to have tried hard to prevent it being put into effect, and Cecil wrote to Archbishop Parker telling him to instruct the bishops not to offer the oath for a second time to anyone without Parker's express approval. Nevertheless, in 1564, in secret, the Bishops of London and Winchester, Edmund Grindal and Robert Horne, tendered the oath for a second time to Bonner, who refused it. Bonner was put on trial for the capital offence of twice denying Elizabeth I's supremacy, something which, as a Catholic, he was obliged to do. In the end the prosecution was dropped and it is reasonable to assume that this was done on royal instruction, although the strong defence put up by Bonner's extremely able Catholic defence lawyer, Edmund Plowden, may also have been a factor. Plowden claimed that the 1559 Act of Supremacy, on which the 1563 Act was based, was not legally enacted since it did not have the support of the bishops in the House of Lords. Second, he argued that Horne, who had administered the oath to Bonner, had not been legally consecrated bishop, because Archbishop Parker, who had made Horne a bishop, had not himself been legally ordained Archbishop of Canterbury in 1559, when the Catholic ex-bishops had refused to play a part in his ordination. This was a touchy matter in view of the claims being made for the continuity between the Church of England and its medieval past. Partly perhaps to avoid too much controversy on this latter point, the case against Bonner was dropped and in 1566–67 parliament passed an Act validating the consecrations of Elizabeth's first bishops but making void prosecutions based on anything done by one of the dubiously ordained bishops. The political decision not to continue with Bonner's prosecution was more decisive than Plowden's clever defence: it is difficult not to see the queen's personal authority behind it.

This leniency towards Catholics in the first decade of the reign did not go unnoticed among Catholic writers at the time, most of whom professed their loyalty to the queen, at least in non-religious matters. Thomas Harding, one of the leading Louvainists, writing in 1567, thanked Elizabeth for her 'advised stay from hasty and sharp persecution', and Thomas Stapleton praised her for her 'clemency'. Even at the end of her reign, one of the Appellant priests wrote a pamphlet defending the proposition that Elizabeth's treatment of Catholics had been 'both mild and merciful'. But the policy of leniency was always under pressure from the more active Protestants in the clergy and among the political elite. The 1563 Act increasing the penalties for denying the royal supremacy and the attempted prosecution of Bonner both show this. Those who tried to persuade Elizabeth to take a tougher line were greatly aided by the Rising of the Northern Earls, the bull of excommunication of 1570 and the international situation, all of which suggested that England was threatened by Catholic forces at home and abroad. The northern rising was suppressed brutally and a number of the Catholic nobility, including the weak but largely loyal Duke of Norfolk, were executed. In addition, three carefully targeted pieces of legislation were passed through parliament in 1570–71. The Treason Act made it treason to deny Elizabeth I's title or to say that she was a heretic, tyrant or usurper; this was clearly a direct reply to the bull of excommunication, which explicitly made these accusations. An Act against Papal Bulls made it treason to bring any papal bull into the country and the Act against Fugitives empowered the government to seize the property of those who fled abroad. What is interesting about these measures, however, is how limited in scope they were. The Fugitives Act was designed to seize the property of those supporters of the Northern Earls who, like the earls themselves, had fled to Scotland and the Spanish Netherlands; it was not a belated effort to deprive the first wave of Catholic migrants who had gone into exile at the beginning of the reign of their posses-sions. The 1570–71 parliament was engaged in the therapeutic, but pointless, exercise of shutting the stable door after the horse has bolted. Moreover, these measures were still not directed against the Catholic community, but only against those members of it who engaged in seditious or treasonous activities.

The development of a harsher anti-Catholic policy after 1580

Everything changed from about 1580, when Elizabeth's policy of leniency gave way to one of persecution. The deteriorating security situation abroad doubtless played a part, as did the fear of sedition, treason and plot at home, but it is important to note that religious considerations were also involved. There seems little doubt that what frightened Elizabeth and her advisers was the development of the missionary movement and of a coherent Catholic policy of open religious resistance among the laity, centring on the practice of recusancy. It looked by 1580 as if the softly-softly policy of killing Catholicism with kindness was not working; indeed Catholicism was undergoing a revival. The revisionist historians' thesis that the seminarists were somehow unimpor-tant or irrelevant in the history of Elizabethan Catholicism was certainly not one shared by Elizabeth and her ministers. The paranoid obsession, which perhaps has added resonance for us in this age of a 'War on Terror', was that the missionary priests carried with them not only the ability to say Mass and perform other Catholic sacraments but also a sinister political message of resistance, rebellion and assassination. This anxiety was well expressed in a pamphlet written by Cecil and printed by the government in 1584 to justify its policy of persecution, *The Execution of Justice in England*. The motive for perse-cuting Catholics was not theological or the result of a desire, like Queen Mary's, to achieve a sort of idealist purity, with everyone holding the same beliefs; it was political.

The government specifically targeted two groups: the recusants and the missionary or seminary priests. The first seminary priest to be executed in England was Cuthbert Mayne in 1577. At that stage there were very few mission-aries in England, and the fact that he was targeted in this way shows an early concern in government about the new movement founded by William Allen. Mayne had gone to Cornwall as the household priest of Francis Tregian, a wealthy member of the gentry, and was convicted under the Act of 1571, which forbade the importation of papal bulls. Yet the bull in Mayne's possession was a religious one, connected with the Jubilee of 1575, and had nothing to do with the 1570 bull of excommunication. Mayne's execution was wide open to criticism since anyone could see that he was not a traitor.

In 1580 Persons, Campion and their Jesuit companions arrived in England amid a great deal of publicity; other missionaries were also coming in large numbers by this time. In 1581 the government arrested Campion and others (Persons escaped abroad) and held a large show trial, charging them with conspiracy to assassinate the queen. The government had to work very hard to secure evidence of a conspiracy, using spies it had sent abroad to infiltrate the seminaries. In fact there was no conspiracy, and the evidence from the spies was concocted, but the government got a conviction and executed the priests.

This rather unsatisfactory state of affairs — there were other similar trials — convinced the government of the need for further legislation, which also allowed parliament to let off steam on the subject of Catholics. One way to contain the Puritans, who had strong support in parliament, was to allow them to attack Catholics and thus show their loyalty to the queen and Protestantism. The result was an Act passed in 1581 'to retain the Queen's Majesty's subjects in their due obedience', which made it treason — and therefore punishable by death — to 'reconcile' someone to the Catholic Church with the intent to withdraw that person from allegiance to the queen, or to be so reconciled. ('Reconciliation' was the technical term for the reconversion of someone whose links to Catholicism had been broken by being associated with the schism of the Church of England.) This Act was reinforced in 1584 by another Act, passed at a time of great international excitement as Europe seemed to be sliding into full-scale war sparked off by the assassination of the Dutch Protestant leader, William of Orange. The 1584 Act made it treason to be found to be a priest in England having been ordained abroad. In other words, if the prosecution could simply show that the accused was a seminary priest, he would be executed. This was blatant religious persecution.

The government now had the means at its disposal to persecute missionary priests. The thinking behind the persecution was to remove the leadership of the Catholic movement and thus stem the development of a Counter-Reformation Catholic sect in England. Behind this was a general feeling that national unity depended on religious unity and a specific fear that Catholic priests were spreading seditious ideas and even plotting to depose the queen and support a Spanish invasion.

It is reckoned that 183 Catholics were killed for their religion in Elizabeth I's reign. Of these, 123 were priests and one was an unordained friar; all but three of those executed were seminary priests; only four were Jesuits, although six more martyrs were received into the Society while in prison. The great majority were executed in the 1580s and 1590s; the peak year for executions was 1588. The method of execution was 'hanging, drawing and quartering': the men were hanged by the neck and cut down while still alive. They were then pinned down before the executioner, who used a knife to cut their chests open, and their internal organs were pulled out and burnt in front of them. Their lifeless bodies were then cut into four and the pieces stuck up on spikes in prominent places where they remained, sometimes for several years.

Elizabeth I's tally of executions was small in comparison with that of her sister (bearing in mind the different length of their reigns) and with the religious persecution in other parts of Europe. Some Catholic priests were tortured to extract information, but others were simply imprisoned and kept in internment camps like Wisbech Castle. Still others, especially in the early 1580s, were deported. In some areas priests seem to have been tolerated by the local Protestant authorities, whether out of neighbourliness, a desire not to antagonise the local community, or because the local magistrates were related to the members of the Catholic laity who were sheltering them.

In addition to these priests, 59 Catholic laymen were also executed, largely for harbouring priests but also, under the Act of 1581, for being reconciled to Catholicism themselves. The 1581 Act further widened the scope of Elizabeth's 1559 settlement by making recusancy punishable with a fine of £20 a month, a considerable increase on the one-shilling-a-week fine payable under the 1559 Act of Uniformity and an indication of how sensitive the government was about the campaign in favour of recusancy being waged by the missionary priests. The year before this Act was passed Robert Persons published his *Brief discourse containing certain reasons why Catholics refuse to go to church*, which strongly advocated recusancy and may explain the subsequent legislation. By the Act against Popish Recusants of 1593, all recusants were confined to within 5 miles of their 'place of usual dwelling' unless they had a licence from a Protestant bishop or justice of the peace to travel. Disobedience was punishable by the forfeiture of all goods for life; recusants who publicly gave up Catholicism, however, were to be pardoned.

The fine of £20 a month imposed in 1581 was well beyond the pocket of most people; it was clearly meant to hit the rich, and since they are generally reckoned to have been the backbone of the Catholic revival, the fine was a clever way of trying to deter these leading figures in Tudor society from failing to come to church. It was also a useful form of taxation, at a time when the Exchequer was suffering from the effects of an expensive foreign policy: between 1581 and 1592 it is calculated that £45,000, roughly a third of the government's ordinary annual income, was raised from fewer than 200 individual recusants.

By the end of the reign, the persecution of Catholics was less sharp. The war with Spain was coming to an end, and peace was returning to Europe. A few Catholic priests continued to be arrested and executed every year and the rich were still paying their exorbitant fines, but once again the fairly gentle instincts of the Elizabethan regime were beginning to reassert themselves. It is reasonable to suggest that the harsh persecution of Elizabethan Catholics had to some degree succeeded in driving Catholics underground and that, as Elizabeth had foreseen, it had also served to strengthen the faith of more resolute and dedicated Catholics. The missionaries became more cautious and retreated into the manor houses of the upper classes or simply remained abroad, writing and building an exile community in Rome, France, Spain and the Netherlands. The Catholic laity also backed off, into a world of subterfuge and anonymity, practising occasional conformity if they lacked the means or the willpower to confront the Protestant establishment head-on.

In the early years of her reign, Elizabeth I had developed the first suggestions in English history of a policy of religious tolerance. Although she shied away from it in the middle years, she had set an important precedent, unusual in Europe, though the Peace of Augsburg of 1555 may have influenced her. Above all, this attempt at tolerance seems to have been associated with the queen herself: many of her chief supporters had deep misgivings. In the end, these councillors succeeded in getting her to abandon this policy, but by the end of the reign, as peace broke out all over Europe, it began to reassert itself. Elizabeth I's great religious contribution to English history may perhaps be seen as the initial hesitant statement of the case for religious toleration.

Questions

1 Was Elizabeth I's initial policy towards Catholics over-optimistic?

2 Who drove Elizabethan policy towards Catholics?

3 Is it accurate to see the survival of English Catholicism as part of the European Counter-Reformation?

How popular had the Elizabethan Church become by the end of the reign?

The Elizabethan religious settlement was not simply the product of two Acts of Parliament passed in 1559; it was the result of a long process that lasted throughout the reign and continued for the next half-century after Elizabeth I's death in 1603. One description of the Elizabethan Church offered for many years by historians and also used by contemporaries was that Elizabeth established a *via media*, a middle way. The difficulty with this description is that we need to know what the Church of England was a compromise *between*: if we mean that the Elizabethan Church was intended to be a halfway house between Roman Catholicism and Protestantism, we would be badly mistaken. Despite the complaints of Puritans and some of the idiosyncrasies of the queen herself, her Church was very far from being Catholic and was acknowledged by all as Protestant. The queen decisively rejected the authority of the pope and this rejection was thoroughly reciprocated in 1570 when he excommunicated her. The Church of England was firmly rooted in the tradition of religious reformation started by Luther and continued by Zwingli and Calvin, and their successors clearly acknowledged this in the support they gave to the Elizabethan Church.

However, if by talking of a middle way we mean that the Church of England had a distinctive character, different from the reformed churches abroad, which positioned it on the 'right wing' of the Protestant tradition, with some aspects reminiscent of the medieval Church that it replaced, then we are on firmer ground. As the Puritans never ceased to complain, some ceremonies were more Catholic than reformed and the Church retained its bishops and medieval courts, which still used the old Catholic canon law. The Elizabethan Church was 'but half reformed', to use the standard Puritan complaint; or, in the more favourable view of Archbishop Matthew Parker, it was a 'reverent mediocrity'.

In the nineteenth century the term 'Anglican' came into wide usage to describe this moderate Protestantism of the Church of England, and some modern historians have used this word to describe the quality of English compromise, which is a distinctive feature of Elizabeth's Church. The word 'Anglican' was not unheard of in the early modern period; the Latin phrase *'ecclesia anglicana'* was commonly used in the Middle Ages to describe the Catholic Church in England: it is used, for example, in Magna Carta. Nevertheless, historians are a little reluctant to use the word 'Anglican' for the Elizabethan period, although it can be a useful shorthand term. Whatever term we use for it, however, a conservative, moderate Protestantism did develop in Elizabeth I's reign. By 1603, when the queen died, this version of reformed Christianity was acquiring a degree of confidence and had the acquiescence, if not the full-blooded support, of the great majority of the English people. We will now look at the reasons for this.

The challenges to the Elizabethan Church

Much of what has been said in this book establishes a case for arguing that Elizabeth I's religious policy would face many obstacles. First, and for Catholic and revisionist historians it is the most significant point, at the outset of the reign England was a Catholic country: there was a deep-rooted loyalty to Catholic forms of worship and a Catholic culture. This may have extended, among the literate minority of the population and many of the clergy, to an acceptance of Catholic theology. More important, perhaps, was the survival among the predominantly rural population of Catholic practices and beliefs that were inherently attractive and fully integrated into the everyday lives of the people. The Catholic calendar of saints' days, feasts and holidays gave a structure to people's lives. In the towns 'mystery' or 'miracle' plays were a popular way of instructing people in Catholic religious stories and were firmly integrated into the social structure of guilds and trades. Late-medieval Catholicism was a religion that appealed to the senses of a largely illiterate and uneducated population, strongly attached to the images that decorated the church and to the complex ceremonial of the Catholic rite. It is impossible to say how popular and deep-rooted this traditional religion really was, especially in the light of the battering it had received since 1529 from reforming clergymen and two reforming kings, but the revisionist historian would argue that this 'survivalism' represented a considerable challenge to the successful establishment of

Protestantism. Add to this the Catholic challenge presented by the growth later in the reign of a Counter-Reformation missionary movement and we have a considerable threat to Elizabethan Protestantism, especially in the north of England.

Every religion is an exercise in education as well as worship, and one generation needs to hand on to the next the fundamentals of the faith. Arguably, this was the greatest challenge to Elizabeth I's religion, especially at the beginning of her reign. One problem was that the number of people prepared to put themselves forward for a career in the Church had declined. The dissolution of the monasteries, where many of the candidates for the priesthood had been educated, the intermittent purges of nonconformist parish clergy under successive rulers, not to mention a highly sensible feeling among parents that a career in the Church was not a secure proposition, all meant that ordinations went into decline. As a result, the task of educating people in Christianity was falling by the wayside by the time Elizabeth I came to the throne.

The religious changes of the 30 years before 1558 had led to a 'pick-and-mix' approach to religious belief, with a certain amount of confusion among the less theologically sophisticated of the population about what was really required of them. Into this religious vacuum swarmed a host of strange religious and superstitious beliefs, memorably described in 1971 by Keith Thomas in his highly readable book *Religion and the Decline of Magic*. Thomas argued that the replacement of the lavish, sensuous late-medieval Catholicism by a dour, intellectual Protestantism in the Tudor period encouraged the growth of a bewildering range of superstitious beliefs, which shaped the ordinary lives of the rural population until the industrialisation and urbanisation of the modern age swept them away. Thomas was able to provide much evidence for continued belief, well after the Reformation, in witchcraft, folk medicine, soothsaying and prophecy, astrology, ghosts and fairies, all replacing what Thomas called the 'magic of the medieval church'. Thomas's central thesis presents something of a challenge to, while also presumably to some extent inspiring, the Catholic revisionist school of Reformation history. However, the challenge for any religion, whether the pre-Reformation Catholicism or the new Protestantism, was how to counteract this tendency towards superstition while at the same time integrating acceptable popular beliefs and practices into its doctrine; both Catholics and Protestants, for example, were prepared to accept that it was necessary to burn witches. Nor should we forget that group of English men and women who have been rather neglected by earnest modern historians: those who were not religious at all and were more attracted by the culture of the alehouse and a spirit of freedom, an attitude which the religious uncertainty of the period could only encourage.

Finally, Elizabethan Protestants ran the risk that if they moderated their approach in order to accommodate rural Catholics, they might lose control of the extreme Protestants, Puritans and separatists, in the towns. In the long run this was to be Anglicanism's greatest challenge and one which it largely lost. However, while this was a problem among the academics of Elizabethan Oxford and Cambridge and the intellectuals at court and in parliament, it was less significant at parish level. Puritanism was generally an ally to Protestants fighting to convert England.

The Elizabethan Church's advantages

Elizabeth I's new Church had a number of distinct advantages. First and foremost, the support of the queen and, in the end, of the greater part of the political establishment, at court, in the Privy Council and in parliament, was crucial. The length of Elizabeth I's reign, 45 years — the longest reign since Edward III in the fourteenth century — enabled her moderate brand of Protestantism to settle; by the time she died, the majority of the population could scarcely remember any other sort of religion. Historians also argue, persuasively, that the support given by Puritans to the Anglican settlement was significant. However, this was a two-way street: Elizabeth refused (or felt forced to refuse) to allow the anti-Puritans among her councillors to follow up their victories over the Puritans in the 1570s and 1580s; indeed, she allowed moderate Puritans to influence religious policy. In return, the Puritans refused to be drawn into separatism and supported the establishment in the battle to convert the country. A number of reasons have been advanced for the willingness of Puritans to cooperate with the establishment of Anglicanism. Puritans saw themselves as part of the broad European reforming tradition stretching back to Luther. The Calvinist doctrine of predestination, the belief that God has long ago decided who will go to heaven and who will go to hell, was a significant part of both the theology of the Elizabethan Church and of the Puritans. Predestination was referred to in the Thirty-Nine Articles and repeated in the Lambeth Articles of 1593, published by that 'Puritan-finder general', Archbishop Whitgift. Nicholas Tyacke argues persuasively that it was predestination that bound the Protestant tradition together until a generation after Elizabeth I's death, when it was undermined by the new doctrine imported from Holland called Arminianism, which led to a catastrophic falling-out between Anglicans and Puritans and contributed significantly to the outbreak of civil war in 1642. Some historians have expressed their doubts about this thesis: Arminian views were already being expressed in the later years of

Elizabeth I's reign and in any case the doctrine of predestination was complex and much debated among Protestants of all sorts at the time. The broader point is certainly acceptable: by and large there were no significant metaphysical debates within the Elizabethan Protestant tradition — it was over church government and ritual that Puritans and conservatives disagreed.

A second important factor that bound Puritans and Protestants together was their opposition to Catholicism. Puritan leaders, such as Cartwright, and their opponents on the conservative wing of the Church, such as Parker, contributed to the substantial literature opposing the power of the pope and other core Catholic beliefs. In fact, there was a sort of rivalry between them to see who could be the more anti-Catholic. At the same time, Puritans and Protestants shared a rejection of unorthodox political ideas: they both supported the theory of 'non-resistance' — the belief that royal authority was to be obeyed, not resisted. The wider political context also meant that Puritans tended to support Elizabeth. As the threat of Catholic insurgency grew, it was the Puritans who were among the strongest advocates of the persecution of Catholic missionary priests and recusants. In the parliaments of the 1570s and 1580s, Puritans were willing to make concessions in their programme of church reform as long as they got concessions in return. These included a harsher attitude towards Catholics, both in terms of persecution and of gestures like the 1584 Bond of Association, by which the queen's Protestant supporters bound themselves in an alliance to murder the imprisoned Mary, Queen of Scots if Elizabeth herself were assassinated.

However, it was above all in the war with Spain in the 1580s and 1590s and in the commitment of English forces to support Protestants in France, Scotland and the Netherlands that Elizabeth found herself most strongly supported by Puritans. The acceptance of the need for this active foreign policy was perhaps the lasting achievement of the Puritans and one which, for many of them, was worth the sacrifice of a few of their proposals for liturgical or ecclesiastical reform.

Many Protestants who were dissatisfied with the settlement of 1559 comforted themselves with the belief that there would be gradual improvements if they would only wait for royal policy to develop. An important concept, which reconciled these moderate Puritans to the slow pace of religious change, was the idea that matters of ritual, ornaments and vestments were *adiaphora*, a Greek word meaning 'things indifferent' or non-essential. It meant that disputes over the use of the surplice or the crucifix were unnecessary, because they were not theologically central, and hence it was reasonable to obey the royal line in such matters. Adiaphorism had been appealed to by moderates in the reign of Edward VI and it was a significant aspect of the Anglican *via media*, which helped draw together the different wings of Protantism.

The gradual expansion of Protestantism under Elizabeth I

The work of converting the confused and superstitious people of Elizabethan England to the moderate Protestantism of its newly established Church took time and was hardly complete even by 1603. In a sense it would never be, since the process was a continuous one, conducted against the backdrop of a rapidly growing population. At the top was the leadership of a committed body of bishops. These men were probably less self-serving and more modest in their pretensions than their late medieval Catholic counterparts had been. Many had been in exile under Mary I and were zealous and devout Protestants, often on very good terms with people we now call Puritans.

Elizabeth I's reign started with the Act of Exchange, which seemed to threaten the remaining wealth of the bishops with confiscation by the Crown, but Elizabeth did not pursue a policy of plunder and, in theory at least, the bishops' wealthy endowments could be used to support the expansion of the Protestant religion. Elizabeth was sometimes slow to replace bishops when they died; the bishopric of Oxford remained vacant for most of her reign in order for the Crown to draw the income of the see, as was the Crown's right when a vacancy occurred.

Although they were under the close supervision of the Privy Council and the archbishops, Elizabeth's bishops were generally free to function as they liked except that, apart from intermittent attendance at parliament, they were expected to perform religious rather than political duties; the only bishop to have a political role under Elizabeth was Archbishop Whitgift. Without political responsibilities, bishops could devote more time to supervising their dioceses. The integration of the bishops into the wider Elizabethan social and political system continued, though mainly at local or regional level. At the top the Church was supervised by the Court of High Commission, composed of both lay and clerical members, an indication of the support the senior clergy received from, but also of their subordinate role to, the lay political elite.

The real agents of religious change in the Elizabethan Church were the clergy, who ran the roughly 10,000 parishes into which the country was divided. At the beginning of the reign, the commissioners who enforced the settlement of 1559 had generally been lenient in rooting out Catholic-sympathising parish priests who were half-hearted about the new religion. Figures are difficult to come by but estimates indicate that about 500 clergy were either forced to resign or did so willingly in 1558–60, with perhaps a similar number leaving over the next 10 years as the pressure on them to conform was gradually increased. From one point of view this presented the new Church with a real problem: it meant that a sizeable number of parishes lacked a resident clergyman. Clergy from neighbouring parishes had to attempt to minister to the religious needs of the villagers, laying themselves open to the accusation (largely from later historians) of being non-resident or 'pluralist', i.e. taking more than one position in the Church for material gain.

The relatively small number of forced and unforced resignations among the lower clergy suggests that the first generation of Elizabethan clergy, especially those ordained under Mary I and Henry VIII, were likely to be instructing their flocks in a very lukewarm form of Protestantism. This does much to explain why 'church papists' — Catholics who continued to attend the established Church — were such a feature of the religious history of the early years of the reign. Slow compliance with Elizabeth I's religious injunctions, of which there is also good evidence from all over the country, can clearly be explained by the survival of Catholic priests on the payroll of the Elizabethan Church. On the other hand, this lack of enthusiasm at parish level also proved a positive feature for Elizabeth: it meant that the process of conversion from Catholicism to Protestantism, while it might be slow, would be more likely to take effect. The village populations in backward areas were weaned away from the old faith by the slow withering away of their Catholic clergy and by the reluctant conformism of the priests who decided to stay on.

Gradually, a new breed of committed, sometimes Puritan, clergy replaced the older generation. The Tudor period saw an extension of educational facilities, especially the grammar schools founded by the Crown or by wealthy benefactors. The Universities of Oxford and Cambridge recovered slowly from the impact of the dissolution of the monasteries but developed in Elizabeth I's reign as training centres for Protestant clergy. Sir Walter Mildmay, Elizabeth's Puritan-minded chancellor of the exchequer, founded Emmanuel College, Cambridge in 1586, specifically as a seminary for Church of England ministers, and the Countess of Sussex endowed a similar institution at Cambridge, which became Sydney Sussex College. By the end of the reign, it is estimated that 40% of the clergy were graduates, a significant increase on late-medieval figures. Above all, by 1603 the parish churches of England were more or less fully manned and virtually none of the clergy who had been ordained before 1558 was still in post. There even seems to have been a surplus of clergy: they were found additional employment in the growth of the 'lectureship', a post endowed by wealthy laypeople, especially in the more 'godly' towns, specifically for preaching sermons.

The duties of the parish clergy most closely connected with the expansion of Protestantism were catechising, preaching and performing the sacraments.

Clergy were expected to school the children and unlearned adults of the parish in the elements of the Christian faith. To help them there was a catechism, a book containing a series of questions and answers on Christianity that students were expected to learn by heart. Christopher Marsh has suggested that, as the Catholic practice of individual confession declined, it was replaced as an educational tool by the use of the catechism. The official catechism used in the Elizabethan Church limited itself to the fundamentals of the Christian religion and avoided entering the controversies between Catholics or Protestants. It could be argued that this made the transition from Catholicism to Protestantism smoother, as parents were more willing to allow their children to be catechised through a non-controversial format. In addition to the official catechism, a minor industry developed in publishing other similar works, which sold widely and were used by the heads of households with living-in apprentices, maidservants and others who worked on the farm or in the workshop. The Church also published its own Primer, a more advanced religious textbook for use in schools, which on close inspection proves quite Puritan in its doctrine.

Once his parishioners had been taught the main elements of the Christian faith, the work of the clergyman was to reinforce their beliefs and mould their behaviour through preaching. It is often said that Protestantism laid greater stress on preaching than Catholicism did, and some of the early English reformers, notably Hugh Latimer, had been stirring preachers. One problem was that many of the parish clergy were insufficiently intelligent or educated (or both) to preach; moreover, some conservative members of the ruling classes suspected that these ministers of religion might be preaching seditious or extreme religious and political ideas. The queen herself took this view and in one of her quarrels with Archbishop Grindal told him that no more than three or four preachers were required in each shire. Clergymen needed a certificate from their bishop before they could preach; clergy who lacked certificates were ordered to read to their congregations from an official book of sermons called the *Book of Homilies* and based on the earlier Edwardian book that was substantially the work of Cranmer. The homilies were studiously conservative and dealt largely with moral and social questions rather than religious controversy; in any case, reading out of a book of sermons is a poor substitute for the lively preaching of a learned, 'godly' man. Much of the effort of the Puritans in Elizabeth I's reign was concentrated on developing the education and in-service training of the clergy, through prophesyings and, in the 'godly' towns and larger villages, through endowed lectureships. The more committed lay folk in Elizabethan England would travel some distance to hear a good sermon, and 'gadding' to sermons became something of a fashion.

The clergyman's main responsibility, however, was to administer the sacraments: to conduct the Sunday services and perform baptisms, marriages and burials. It has been argued that the use of English rather than the Latin of the Catholic Mass was an important factor in winning people over to the Protestant Church. The language of the Elizabethan Prayer Book, based on the Edwardian translation of Cranmer, was both poetic and accessible to the increasingly educated and literate laity. The churches of post-Reformation England may have seemed less visually attractive without their clutter of medieval imagery (itself presumably a matter of taste), but the ritual of Protestantism was both attractive and comprehensible to the people. The Lutheran tradition of singing psalms in translation and the use of music in church made the services less drab than is sometimes suggested by Catholic historians. The English Bible and its central role in the Sunday service was also a significant factor, although the production of a definitive, official translation had to wait until the Authorised Version of James I. The availability of a Welsh Prayer Book and eventually of a Welsh translation of the Bible was significant in preventing the Catholic faith from retaining its grip in Wales.

To back up the work of Protestant catechising, teaching and preaching, the Elizabethan printing press was used extensively. A sizeable number of books printed in Europe for at least two centuries after the invention of printing in the 1450s were religious, and in England the press was closely controlled by the Stationers' Company under the supervision of the government. Catholics also published about 300 separate religious titles in Elizabeth I's reign, though they were almost all printed abroad and then smuggled into the country. Ownership of Catholic books could be dangerous. Very few Catholic books were printed in England, of which the most notable was the book that became known as Edmund Campion's 'Brag' of 1580, but this was done in secret and at great risk to the printers, who needed to move their press around the country to avoid arrest. Similarly, a few extreme Puritan publications were printed in England, especially the scurrilous 'Martin Marprelate' pamphlets of 1588–89, but again this was done secretly, away from London in a press set up in the houses of Puritan sympathisers. Other radical Protestant works were printed abroad and smuggled in, such as the works of 'H. N.', the Dutch leader of the Family of Love. When the suspected authors, publishers and smugglers of these books were discovered by the government, they risked being executed, as happened to 'Martin Marprelate'. Overall, the spread of Protestantism was helped by the strict censorship of the press.

Religious books included learned works of theological controversy written in Latin by bishops or academics; works of devotion containing prayers; catechisms; and a large popular literature of ballads and 'chap books', which often contained simplified religious propaganda for those who wanted lighter — and cheaper — reading matter. A growing number of people could read, and the spread of printing, especially in the vernacular, encouraged this process. However, it is still probably the case that more than half the population, especially women, could not read, and although they could listen to others reading out loud — a common practice at the time — this must have made the task of converting the English people more difficult.

The Protestant Church in Elizabeth I's reign produced a number of outstanding religious works. In 1563 John Foxe published the first full English edition of his *Acts and Monuments* or 'Book of Martyrs' as it became known (the title page is reproduced on p. 93 plus commentary). This was, after the translated Bible and Prayer Book, the most important religious book ever printed in English. Foxe had collected together accounts of all the Protestants killed by Queen Mary, and published them in all their gory detail, accompanied by gruesome pictures. The book was an instant best-seller and went through numerous editions during Elizabeth I's reign and beyond. Foxe showed his Protestant martyrs as courageous heroes and their Catholic enemies as cruel bigots. One significant theme running through the book at an almost subconscious level was the idea that the English were God's 'elect nation', like the Israelites of the Old Testament. The association of Protestantism with patriotism and of Catholicism with foreign threats was an important part of the way in which the new Church established itself. Foxe's book was organised around the highly significant idea that the Protestants who were burnt at the stake in Mary I's reign were part of a religious tradition that stretched back to the earliest days of church history, when Christians were persecuted by Roman emperors. Hence the Church established in 1559 could trace itself back to the Children of Israel of the Old Testament and was not some new-fangled institution created by religious innovators.

This important point was rammed home in another work published in 1563, *An Apology for the Church of England*, by Bishop John Jewel. Jewel's brief work appeared both in Latin (for a foreign audience) and in English and its purpose was to defend, or 'apologise' for, his Church in the face of Catholic attacks. Jewel argued that Protestantism was no new heresy but the true Christian faith, which had for centuries suffered under the tyranny of the pope but was now released by the efforts of reformers.

The fullest defence of the Church of England appeared in 1593 when Richard Hooker produced his long and learned work, *Of the Laws of Ecclesiastical Polity*. Hooker essentially repeated the points made by Foxe and Jewel, but he defended the Church from attacks by Puritans as well as Catholics, thereby establishing a reasoned case for the *via media* of the

Elizabethan Church. Hooker also produced a philosophical defence of the royal supremacy and the use of bishops, rather than the Presbyterian system that many Puritans wanted.

How Protestant had England become by 1603?

It is impossible to be precise about how far the new Church of England had succeeded by 1603 in converting England to its views, but there is general agreement among historians that it had largely done so. An interesting, though difficult, question is when the tipping point occurred. The events of 1569 suggest that it might have come rather earlier in the reign than revisionist historians suggest.

Throughout the Tudor period there were rebellions inspired, in part, by opposition to royal religious policy. The most serious of these was the 1536 Pilgrimage of Grace, a largely Catholic protest against Henry VIII's break with Rome and the dissolution of the monasteries. In 1549 there were two serious uprisings against Edward VI's government, a Catholic one in Devon and Cornwall against the new Prayer Book and Ket's Rebellion in East Anglia, though Ket's rebels used in their great camp near Norwich the very Prayer Book that the rebels in the West Country so disliked. In 1554 Wyatt's Rebellion in Kent was a Protestant revolt against Queen Mary. All these uprisings failed, but even so, each was a more serious affair than the Rising of the Northern Earls of 1569, the only religious rebellion that Elizabeth I faced. After a decade of reluctant conformity to the Elizabethan settlement, the Earls of Northumberland and Westmorland and Lord Dacre rose in rebellion in the far north of England. Although it also had political and economic causes, the rebellion quickly took on a Catholic tone and when the rebels took Durham they celebrated Mass there, with a seditious priest called William Holmes officiating. That, however, was all they achieved, and Elizabeth crushed the rebellion with notable ruthlessness. In comparison the Pilgrimage of Grace involved almost the entire upper and middle classes of all the counties north of the River Don; the rebels took York, the capital of the north, and forced Henry VIII to give them a pardon, which he more or less kept to, and to modify his religious policy. No change in policy followed 1569 and only a small proportion of the population got involved: the rebellion was a flop.

Catholicism was still considered a political threat after 1569, but there was more paranoia than realism in the government's attitude. There were a number of Catholic plots, Ridolfi (1571), Throckmorton (1583) and Babington (1586), but these were just plots involving small groups, often infiltrated by government spies and exploited by the government as anti-Catholic propaganda. After 1569 several hundred Catholic adventurers left England to fight in the Catholic cause abroad in the European Wars of Religion. Some of them were eventually organised into a regiment set up in the Netherlands by Elizabeth's great enemy, Philip II of Spain. Otherwise, Catholicism after 1569 was a religious, not a political, movement involving a very small part of the population, concentrated in certain parts of the country. It is therefore difficult to see what revisionist historians can mean when they speak of Elizabeth's failure to establish her Church. Their evidence is mainly drawn from detailed, local complaints by disgruntled clergymen faced with troublesome rustics or from the church courts that enforced Church laws. However, medieval history is full of similar complaints about the sinfulness and ignorance of the English and of prosecutions for failure to conform. There is simply not sufficient evidence to speak of a wholesale failure of the Elizabethan Church.

By way of conclusion it is worth attempting a brief tour of Elizabethan England in search of evidence for religious conformity and nonconformity. The strongest Protestant areas were in the south and east. London remained a Protestant stronghold where Puritanism also flourished. The towns of southern England, especially those with a strong trading or industrial economy, were likewise strongly Protestant, but they also harboured more radical groups. In London and the towns of Kent, Essex and East Anglia, there were strong links with Protestantism on the Continent and the refugee communities of Dutch weavers and cloth-workers there were allowed to practise their Calvinist religion unmolested. English merchant communities in northern Europe were also able to practise more advanced forms of Protestantism, and they kept in close contact with home. In the rural hinterland, where there was often a flourishing textile industry, advanced versions of religion were also practised: hence the Puritan *classis* which flourished at Dedham on the Essex/Suffolk border in the 1580s and was linked to similar meetings in the Midlands. On the whole, Catholicism did not flourish in the southeast, East Anglia or London except in odd pockets where a powerful gentry family managed to keep the old faith alive.

Behind this apparent victory of Protestantism there was a surprising degree of diversity. Cambridgeshire, for example, should have been a secure stronghold for Elizabeth's Church, but even here there was resistance, as shown by the lamentations of Richard Greenham, the puritanical vicar of Dry Drayton, who worked tirelessly between 1570 and 1591, putting especial emphasis on catechising and preaching. However, by 1591 he had had enough and left his parish complaining of 'the intractableness and unteachableness of the people amongst whom he had taken such great pains'. Even in Cambridge itself, the cradle of the Henrician Reformation, the churchwardens of Great St Mary's did not sell their Catholic vestments and plate until 1568, and in the parish of Holy Trinity the altar stone was not disposed of until 15 years after Elizabeth I's accession. In Balsham and Wisbech there was a resilient cell of the Family of Love. There were even revivalist Catholics among the Cambridgeshire gentry, such as the Huddlestons of Sawston and the Paris family of Linton. All over eastern England there were Catholic gentry families, often linked by marriage and surviving despite the persecution: the Walpoles in north Norfolk, the Timperleys of Hintlesham near Ipswich, and the Petre and Wiseman families in Essex. Where there was a Catholic gentry family, there was usually a small Catholic community, composed of their tenants and servants. There is also some evidence that there tended to be more Protestant nonconformists in such areas too, since there would be less social pressure from the lord of the manor to support the established Church.

In the west of England one might assume that Catholicism would survive easily, so far from London and, at least in Devon and Cornwall, with a tradition of resistance to the imposition of Protestantism. However, although old practices survived here long after Elizabeth I's accession, the west of England did not prove fertile ground for a sustained Catholic revival. Perhaps because of the history of Catholic resistance in Cornwall, the authorities were at their most vigilant there. The first execution of a seminary priest, Cuthbert Mayne in 1577, took place in Cornwall, and his trial was accompanied by a campaign against the leading Catholic gentry families, especially the Tregians and Arundells, led by local loyalists such as Richard Grenville and Sir George Carey, who stood to benefit personally by taking over the revenues of any confiscated lands. These Cornish Catholic gentry families survived, sending their sons abroad to be educated in the Catholic schools and seminaries, but gentry Catholicism was more of an elite secret society than anything with the potential to shake the foundations of the new national religion.

In Wales, the publication of the Welsh Prayer Book and Bible helped establish Protestantism in Welsh-speaking areas. It was also politic that 13 of the 16 bishops appointed in Wales under Elizabeth were Welshmen. Catholicism did show itself in Wales: about 100 Welsh students went abroad to be trained as Catholic missionaries and 64 of them were sent on the mission, though only a small number returned to Wales, which bears out Christopher Haigh's criticism that the Catholic missionary movement failed to capitalise on the areas where traditional opposition to Protestantism might be strong. Nevertheless, Welsh Catholicism had certainly not completely perished by 1603: at the beginning of James I's reign a survey of recusants found a higher proportion of recusants to churchgoers in the diocese of Llandaff than in any other diocese. Even so, the numbers were not huge: in the whole of Wales there were only 808 avowed recusants out of a total churchgoing population of 212,450. The general picture of Catholicism in Wales is one of steady decline, slower perhaps than in other parts of the country. There were curiously few Puritans in Elizabethan Wales, although Wales did produce one major Puritan figure in the person of John Penry, hanged in 1593 for his involvement in printing the 'Martin Marprelate' pamphlets. As with the Welsh Catholic semi-narists, Penry did most of his work in England.

The north of England was the chief stronghold of Catholicism in Elizabeth I's reign. It had produced the strongest resistance to Henry VIII's religious changes and in 1569 it was the scene of the only serious rebellion against Elizabeth I's. Nevertheless, the progress of the Reformation in the north under Elizabeth was impressive. As in the Midlands and the south, it was in the towns that Protestantism and some Puritanism spread. Broadly speaking, the northeast was more receptive to the Elizabethan Church, the northwest less so. The strongest centre of Catholicism in Elizabethan England was Lancashire, the home of William Allen, the leader of the Elizabethan Catholics. Christopher Haigh, the historian of Tudor Lancashire's religion, ascribes the strength of Catholicism there to the weakness of the bishopric of Chester, a new diocese created by Henry VIII and poorly endowed; to the poverty and small size of the parishes; and (perhaps contradictorily) to a Catholic revival under Mary I. However, strong Catholicism remained confined to certain areas of the county, where a density of support created a sense of solidarity and mutual encour-agement. A 1604 visitation revealed that 6.2% of the population of churchgoing age in Lancashire were recusants. This compared with only 1.2% in Yorkshire. In the large Lancashire parish of Prescot recusants amounted to 34% of the total. Moreover, there was a significant but unquantifiable population of 'church papists', who would be counted among the churchgoing population. No wonder that James I said, 'at our first entering to this Crown and Kingdom we were informed, and that too truly, that our county of Lancaster abounded more in popish recusants than any other country in England'. In Lancashire towns such as Manchester and Bolton, 'the Geneva of the north', there was a different picture: here Protestantism, and even a smattering of Puritanism, flourished.

It is not possible to summarise here all the important local studies that have recently cast new light on the question of how well-received Elizabeth I's Church was. The broad picture that emerges is as follows: it is impossible to deny that, in one way or another, most of England had become Protestant, even 'Anglican', by 1603. Many people were reluctant converts, or nominal rather than whole-hearted supporters, and there was a significant minority who had decided to separate themselves from the Elizabethan Church, either as 'popish' recusants, the largest group, or as radical Protestant separatists.

The adherents of the Protestant Church were not a coherent body, but rather a spectrum of believers spreading from a Puritan wing at one extreme to a conservative or Anglican one at the other. These different groups were found in different proportions around the country, and historians who look at a particular town or county find diversity even in this small compass: there were Catholics in London and Puritans in Lancashire. Elizabeth I's reign saw a settlement of religion of a sort, but how stable it was, and how well it would survive, only time would tell.

Questions

1 To what extent was the Elizabethan Reformation a battle between town and country?

2 To what extent could it be said that, by 1603, only the educated would go to heaven?

3 Did Elizabeth I have a coherent religious policy over the course of her reign?

Illustrations

The title page of John Foxe's
Acts and Monuments, 1563

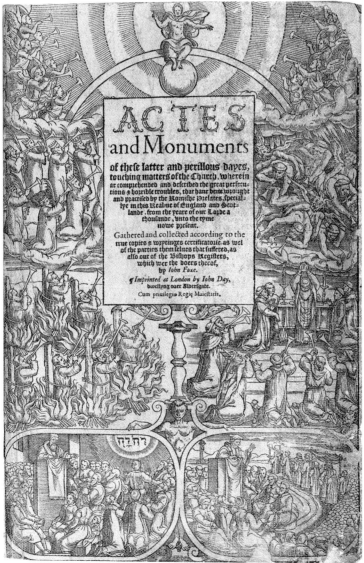

This is the title page of the first full edition of Foxe's famous work. He had spent the reign of Queen Mary in exile, collecting eyewitness accounts of the trials and executions of Protestants. Although Foxe was not an uncritical historian, and certainly made no attempt to be unbiased, it is generally agreed that his account of the Marian persecution is valuable. Foxe's book was one of the great Protestant publications of Elizabeth I's reign, and remained a best-seller until Victorian times, when it was popularly known as Foxe's 'Book of Martyrs'. Foxe's martyrology mostly celebrated the heroism of the Protestants executed by Queen Mary but the book included all Christians unjustly killed for their faith, from the days of the early church onwards. Martyrdom established the authenticity of Protestant beliefs and the cruelty and wickedness of the Catholic tormentors. The book's success owed much to its use of illustrations; the imagery of this title page gives a flavour.

At the end of Elizabeth I's reign the great Jesuit author, Robert Persons, published a lengthy and scholarly work designed to attack the accuracy and truthfulness of Foxe's book. Persons contrasted the 'genuine' martyrdoms of Catholics with the 'pseudo-martyrdom' of Foxe's heroes, in much the same way that Foxe does on this title page, although in Persons' case the roles of saints and devils were reversed.

On the left of the title page illustration are the 'saints', the chosen people of God, in other words the English Protestants and their predecessors. At the bottom is a pious reformed congregation. The minister, not differentiated from his flock by vestments, preaches from the pulpit, while the pious layfolk consult their Bibles. Further up are the martyrs whom John Foxe commemorates in his book. As they are burned in the persecution under Queen Mary, the martyrs are already equipped with their angelic trumpets. At the next level the martyred saints carry the palm leaves of pilgrimage and triumph. At the top is the angelic host in heaven itself. So, the saints on earth, the martyrs at the moment of their death and the angels in heaven are united in their reformed orthodoxy.

The other side of the page, on the right, is a very different picture. At the bottom is a Catholic congregation, worshipping in idolatrous fashion, with their rosaries very much in evidence. The priest is fully vested. To one side a group of the clergy process, also wearing their vestments and carrying crosses. At the next level tonsured monks and mitred bishops attend a Catholic Mass, with the priest elevating the Host before the altar. Above them are the damned in hell, writhing around with a selection of evil-looking devils blowing trumpets in support of the Catholic ceremonial below them and turning their backs on the divine figure at the top, whom the Protestants on the other side of the engraving are adoring. The forces of evil on earth and in hell are united in their Catholicism.

Richard Verstegan's *Theatrum crudelitatum*, 1592

Cambridge University Library, U*.4.41(C)

This engraving shows the death of Margaret Clitherow, who was martyred at York in 1586. She was the daughter of Thomas Middleton, a wax-chandler, and she married a butcher, John Clitherow, in 1571. She lived as a Protestant until 1574, when she embraced Catholicism. She was arrested for recusancy and questioned about harbouring Catholic priests in her home. She refused to give her questioners any information, presumably to protect the identity of other Catholics, and was sentenced to death. The time-honoured punishment for refusing to plead in court was known in legal French as *la peine forte et dure* (the strong and hard punishment). As can be seen from the picture, it involved laying the victim on the ground, covering her with a board and then placing heavy weights on top until she was crushed to death.

The picture also shows a priest being suspended by his ankles and a dungeon at the left where a group of prisoners strike classical poses. The Latin text that accompanied the picture reports that Margaret's husband was forced into exile, her children were beaten and the eldest (aged 12) was imprisoned.

The Latin book in which this engraving appeared was first published in Antwerp and went through three more Latin and five French editions. The full title translates as 'The theatre of the cruelties of the heretics of our times'. This brief book contained 20 copper-plate engravings depicting the persecution of Catholics in England under Henry VIII and Elizabeth I, as well as in the Netherlands and France. It concluded with an account of the death of Mary, Queen of Scots.

The author of the text, and probably also engraver of the illustrations, was Richard Verstegan (c. 1550–1640), the grandson of a Dutch merchant who had settled in London. Verstegan attended Christ Church, Oxford, and was then apprenticed to a goldsmith in London, which may help explain his later skill as an engraver. Verstegan was a Catholic and he was imprisoned in 1578 for printing Catholic books. He went into exile in 1582 and, after travelling around Europe, settled in Antwerp, where he kept in close contact with the leading Elizabethan Catholic exile, Robert Persons.

Verstegan's book is a good example of Catholic martyrology. Its purpose for its Catholic readers was the same as Foxe's for his Protestant ones: to encourage them to stay firm in their faith in the face of persecution. It was also designed for a Catholic readership in Europe, where English exiles lived in constant need of financial aid and where they sought to drum up political support for the 'enterprise of England', a Catholic (probably Spanish) invasion of their heretic country. It is interesting how Verstegan seeks here to link the troubles of English Catholics with the persecution suffered by their co-religionists in Europe: England is seen as part of the Wars of Religion, the struggle between Reformation and Counter-Reformation. It should be added that the story of Margaret Clitherow, as presented by Verstegan, is true.

Portrait of the family of John Towneley, 1601

This John about the 6 or 7 yere of her mᵗⁱᵉ ŷ now ŷs, for professing ŷ apostolical catholick Romaine faith, was imprisoned first at Chester castell, then sent to marshelsea, then to yorke castell, the to ŷ blockhouses in hull, then to the Gatehouse in westminster, then to manchester, then to broughton in oxeforthshire, then twice to Elie in Cambrigeth, and so now of 73 yeares old and blinde, is bounde to appeare and to kepe with in five myles of towneley his houle, who hath since ŷ statut of 23. paid in to ŷ exchequer xx.ᵗⁱ monath: doth still, ŷ there is paid allready above five m . 160

John Towneley is shown kneeling at prayer with his seven sons behind him. They face his wife and her seven daughters. The men are soberly and modestly dressed, the women are a little more flamboyant. The image of a large family devoutly at prayer could represent Puritan piety, until we look more closely and observe the crucifix placed on the lectern. This is a Catholic family, the famous Towneleys of Towneley Hall, Burnley, in Lancashire, at the heart of what Lord Burghley called 'the sink of popery'. They were proud of their gentry ancestry: the shields above the group are the Towneley coats of arms and those of their ancestors and relatives. The picture hung in Towneley Hall until the early twentieth century, doubtless alongside other family portraits. It is a piece of family martyrology and records the suffering of John Towneley in the inscription at the foot of the painting:

> This John about the 6 or 7 year of her majesty that now is, for professing the apostolical Catholic Roman faith was imprisoned first at Chester Castle, then sent to Marshalsea [a London prison], then to York Castle, then to the Blockhouses in Hull, then to the Gatehouse in Westminster, then to Manchester, then to Broughton in Oxfordshire, then twice to Ely in Cambridgeshire, and so now of 73 years old and blind, is bound to appear and to keep within five miles of Towneley, his house: who hath since the statute of [1581] paid into the Exchequer £20 the month, and doth still, that there is paid already above £5,000.

This treatment of a leading Catholic layman was not unusual, although John's imprisonment seems to have started quite early in the reign, in 1568, and perhaps calls into question the idea that until the 1580s Elizabeth I's policy towards Catholics was rather lax. The crippling level of fines imposed on the leading recusants after 1581 could only be supported by the most wealthy and, perhaps, those most willing to practise extreme frugality. The mixture of piety, plain dressing and genealogical pride shown in the picture typifies the mentality of the Elizabethan English Catholic movement. The Towneleys were to remain a leading Catholic family for the next four centuries.

Bibliography

A. G. Dickens, *The English Reformation* (1964)

This is *the* classic textbook on the religious history of the sixteenth century. It presents the standard view of the English Reformation as an act of state that nevertheless met a popular demand for reform. As a result, Dickens sees the Reformation as a fairly brief affair that was largely over by the beginning of Elizabeth I's reign. Elizabeth completed the process of reform, mopping up the limited opposition from Catholics with reasonable ease. Dickens was more subtle than his critics sometimes allow, as this passage shows:

> The Elizabethan settlement was less a pacification than a compromise between contending forces which Elizabeth and her Stuart successors failed to reconcile. The gradual consolidation of an Anglican Church must nevertheless be numbered among the achievements of this versatile age.   p. 418, 1974 edition

P. Collinson, *The Elizabethan Puritan Movement* (1967)

This is one of the greatest examples of history writing in the twentieth century. It is always lively, based on primary research of the highest level and written with obvious sympathy for its subject. Collinson's central argument, that there was a coherent, consistent, organised movement in favour of Puritan reform, was attacked as soon as the book was published, but it still commands attention, if not complete agreement. One reason for this is that Collinson presented his argument with great subtlety and sensitivity, as the following quotation shows:

> The terms puritan and Anglican are elusive and intangible, limited in their usefulness to interpret the complexities of English church history between the Elizabethan Settlement and the Civil War. The English Church of this age was a spectrum, in which the ultimate extremes of colour are clear enough, but the intermediate tones merge imperceptibly.   p. 27

C. Haigh, *English Reformations* (1993)

English Reformations is a useful antidote to Dickens and written almost consciously as such. Haigh's great strength is his ability to question most of Dickens' confident and pro-Anglican conclusions about the speed and popularity of the Reformation both in Elizabeth I's reign and in the years before it. Haigh summarises the earlier Catholic revisionism of J. J. Scarisbrick and adds his own, somewhat quirky, revisionist views. His main original contribution is his interpretation of Elizabethan Catholicism, where he underplays the contribution of the Jesuits and seminarists. Broadly, Haigh sees the religious history of the sixteenth century as a matter of failure:

> So the Tudor reformations had not replaced a Catholic England by a Protestant England: the country was divided, and the Protestants were insecure; popery had not been crushed, the worldlings had not turned to the gospel. For the godly, parish Anglicans were not only failed Protestants, they were potential papists; they were still contaminated with Antichrist, unable to reject the devil and his works.   p. 293

C. Marsh, *Popular Religion in Sixteenth-Century England* (1998)

The great emphasis in recent research on Elizabethan religion has been on what might be called the social history of the subject, approaching it especially through local studies. This excellent book sums up the conclusions of this research brilliantly, setting Elizabeth I's reign in its wider Tudor context. In the process, Marsh gives a well-balanced answer to the question posed by revisionist historians, 'How popular was the Elizabethan Reformation?' Marsh's conclusion is that a sort of grudging acceptance best describes how the English welcomed the religious policy of Elizabeth I, as they had the policies of her three predecessors:

> Recent research has left us in little doubt that, broadly speaking, the people of sixteenth-century England responded to official religious commands by doing what they were told. Churchwardens up and down the land snuffed out candles, removed statues and whitewashed walls with remarkable obedience. Then they reversed the whole process in a similar spirit. Then they repeated it once again.   p. 201

P. Marshall, *Reformation England 1480–1642* (2003)

This is a lucid, reliable summary of the state of recent research. Marshall gives a balanced survey of the great controversies of the last half century; the long period covered enables the reader to set Elizabeth I's religious history in its wider context. Marshall insists on the importance of studying both Elizabeth I's reign and that of her successor, James I, in order to understand the English Reformation:

> One insight which draws together many of the divergent approaches to Elizabethan and Jacobean religion in recent scholarship is a recognition that this period belongs at the heart of 'the Reformation' as a unit of meaningful historical analysis, that its religious quarrels and tensions were not, as were once thought, 'residual problems' to be cleared up backstage after the Elizabethan Settlement had brought down the curtain on the main show.   p. 141

Glossary

Anabaptist

a believer in adult, rather than infant, baptism. Anabaptists were regarded as among the most extreme of Protestants.

Anglican

a modern word for a member of the Church of England. The term is sometimes used to describe the moderate Protestants who supported Elizabeth I's *via media* but tended to disagree with the Puritans.

Appellant

a legal term for one who lodges an appeal; used specifically to describe the secular Catholic priests who appealed to the pope in 1598–1603 against the appointment of a pro-Jesuit archpriest to lead the Catholics in England. The Appellants opposed the Jesuits and hoped to gain toleration from Queen Elizabeth I.

archbishop

a senior bishop with authority over other bishops. There are two English archbishops, for the provinces of York and Canterbury. The latter is senior to the former.

Arminian

a follower of the Dutch reformer Jacobus Arminius (1560–1609) who was critical of the Calvinist doctrine of predestination. Arminians in England were at their most active in the reigns of James I and Charles I.

bishop

a senior clergyman with authority over the priests and ministers in his diocese. A bishop's cathedral base is his see. Bishops have authority to ordain priests and conduct the sacrament of confirmation.

Book of Common Prayer

(also known as the Prayer Book) the officially sanctioned and legally enforced service book of the Church of England. The book contains the text of the liturgy for all church services and was designed to replace the text of the Catholic Mass. Different Prayer Books were introduced by the Acts of Uniformity of 1549, 1552 and 1559, that of 1552 being the most radical and that of 1559 representing a compromise between different religious positions.

bull (papal)

a decree issued by the pope. The word comes from the Latin *bulla* for the seal that gave it its authority. Papal bulls are still known by the first few Latin words of their text. The bull by which Elizabeth I was excommunicated in 1570 was called *Regnans in Excelsis*.

Calvinist

a follower of the French Protestant reformer John Calvin (1509–64). Calvin considerably radicalised Martin Luther's reforms by instituting a democratic system of church government, abolishing the rigid distinction between clergy and laity, and introducing a new theology based on belief in predestination. Calvin and his followers were based in the Swiss city of Geneva, from where they exerted a powerful influence on Protestant communities all over Europe, including Protestants and Puritans in England.

catechism

a book used to instruct children and new converts in the fundamentals of the Christian faith. The catechism consists of a series of questions to be put by the priest or minister to the students, to which they are supposed to learn the answers by heart.

Catholic

a member of the Catholic, or Roman Catholic, Church. *Catholic* means 'universal' (and, in lower case, is still used in that sense); its use reflects the Church's claims to global authority and to be the original church founded by Christ, as opposed to the eastern Orthodox Church, from which the Catholic Church split in 1054, and the Protestant Church. The Church of England rejected the authority of the pope but also claimed direct descent from the original church; hence its retention of the Catholic structure of bishops and archbishops and what might otherwise appear its paradoxical description of itself as 'one holy Catholic and apostolic Church'.

Catholic Reformation

a process of renewal and reform within the Catholic Church usually dated to the Council of Trent (1545–63), though some elements of reform were underway long before the council met. The process involved recognising and rejecting many of the abuses that had first been identified by Protestant reformers and instituting new ceremonies and practices to revive and enhance the emotional and spiritual elements within the practice of the Catholic faith. It was closely linked with the Counter-Reformation.

Church of England

the Protestant Anglican Church first established by Henry VIII in 1533–36. Its theology was determined by a series of Acts of Parliament and enshrined in sets of articles and in the text of the Book of Common Prayer.

classis

(plural: *classes*) a meeting of clergymen in a particular area for mutual support and to make decisions on how to run the religious life of their congregations. It was the second level of the Presbyterian or Calvinist church structure.

Communion

also known as the Eucharist, the most important of the religious services in the Christian Church, in which wine is drunk and bread eaten in commemoration of Christ's Last Supper. Catholics believed in transubstantiation, i.e. that the body and blood of Christ were physically present in the bread and wine; for this reason they were offered up at an altar, which is still the focal point of Catholic churches, and received kneeling. Protestant belief varied in its detail but most Protestants rejected the sacrificial idea in favour of a simple act of commemoration; Communion was therefore administered from a simple table. Catholics only distributed the bread, in wafer form, to the laity; the wine was reserved for the priest. Protestants believed in Communion 'in both kinds', with laity and clergy receiving both the bread and wine.

conventicle

gathering of extreme Protestants, such as separatists, outside the official body of the Church of England.

Council of Trent

a general council of the Catholic Church held at Trento in Italy in three sessions between 1545 and 1563. The council instituted the reforms promoted by the Catholic Reformation and the discipline spearheaded by the Counter-Reformation.

Counter-Reformation

the process of reform and evangelism by which the Catholic Church responded to the Protestant Reformation. It was initiated by the Council of Trent and took the form of a process of renewal within the Church, often called the Catholic Reformation, and a policy of asserting the truth of Catholicism in dispute and debate with Protestant leaders. Missionary work was an important part of the Counter-Reformation.

Glossary

Court of High Commission

a court that developed from the Act of Supremacy of 1559 and became the most important church court in the province of Canterbury (there was a separate one in York). Its members were senior clergymen and laymen.

crucifix

an ornament made up of a cross with the image of Christ crucified on it, often found in Catholic churches, but disliked by Puritans.

doctrine

the teaching of a particular church or religion.

Erastian

a type of church in which the clergy are subordinate to lay authority, especially that of the ruler. Named after a Swiss reformer, Thomas Erastus (1524–83), whose ideas were developed in debates with an English supporter of Calvin early in the reign of Elizabeth I.

excommunication

expulsion from a congregation or church. In 1570 Pope Pius V excommunicated Elizabeth I, expelling her from the Catholic Church (which she had already left) and telling her subjects not to obey her.

injunction

an order or detailed instruction. In 1559 Elizabeth I issued injunctions, based on those of Edward VI, explaining in more depth how her Church should be run.

Jesuit

a member of the Society of Jesus founded by the Spaniard Ignatius Loyola (1491–1556). Jesuits were highly educated and trained to take on Protestant theologians in debate. The society gained a reputation for efficiency and a secret network of agents akin to a modern secret service. Jesuits were particularly hated by Protestants and they suffered severe penalties under Elizabethan law.

laity

the non-clerical members of a congregation or church.

liturgy

the words and ceremonies used in church services. The Church of England liturgy is contained in the Book of Common Prayer.

Luther, Martin (1483–1546)

German religious reformer, credited with having started the Reformation. Although his clashes with the papacy were dramatic, involving public debate, political kidnapping, civil war and his own excommunication, Luther's religious ideas on the Eucharist and church organisation and government were surprisingly conservative. Although some areas of northern Europe remained attached to his philosophy, by the 1540s Lutheranism had largely given way to Calvinism.

Mass

the most important Catholic service, which has at its centre the Eucharist. The Mass is essentially a service of sacrifice based around a stone altar, in which the body and blood of Christ are offered up in the form of sanctified bread and wine. Protestants were outraged at the idea that Christ's body could be sacrificed a second time after his death on the cross, and denounced the Mass as a mixture of idolatry and satanic ritual.

pope

the Bishop of Rome, entrusted with authority over the Catholic Church. Catholic tradition maintains that the popes hold their office in a direct line of succession — through the laying-on of hands — from St Peter, the first 'pope'. The papacy claimed authority over the Church in all parts of the world.

predestination

the Calvinist belief that people are destined by God for heaven or hell, and that they cannot change their destiny. Belief that some people were predestined from before birth to go to heaven predated Calvin; his emphasis was on 'double predestination', the idea that some (the elect or godly) are predestined for heaven and everyone else (the ungodly) predestined for hell.

Presbyterian

a supporter of Calvinist ideas on church government and structure. Calvin involved the laity in running individual congregations by means of a consistory court; congregations were linked together in local groups known as *classes* and then organised into regional and national synods. The Presbyterian system elects its ministers and therefore rejects the need for bishops.

prophesying

a meeting of clergymen in a locality, sometimes with a lay audience, designed to improve standards of preaching by instructing less well-educated clergy. Prophesyings were based on meetings first developed by Zwingli and were popular in the 1570s, especially among Puritans.

Protestant

a general term used to describe those who broke away from the Catholic Church in the sixteenth century out of a desire to reform religion. In Elizabethan England it describes all those of a religious outlook who rejected Catholicism, both Puritans and more conservative Anglicans.

quietist

one who wishes to practise religion without disturbing others and without trying to impose his/her beliefs on others.

Puritan

a Protestant who wished to 'purify' the Church of England of the remaining Catholic elements that Elizabeth I had retained in 1559, but who wished to do so from within the Church and did not want to separate him/herself from it.

recusant

one (especially a Catholic) who refused to attend the Protestant church services of the Church of England.

Reformation

improvement, especially in religious matters. The word is applied especially to the European religious movement, which Luther started in 1517 and which resulted in the division of the continent into Catholics and 'reformed' Protestants.

revisionist

a historian who challenges the views of his or her predecessors and tries to present a clearer picture of the past. In the field of Tudor religious history it describes those historians writing in the 1980s and 1990s, notably Christopher Haigh, Eamon Duffy and Jack Scarisbrick, who modified the account given by A. G. Dickens of the English Reformation.

sacrament

a ritual in the Catholic Church whose performance enhances the receiver's chances of going to heaven. Catholics recognise seven sacraments: baptism, penance or confession (nowadays known as reconciliation), Communion, confirmation, matrimony, holy orders (becoming a Catholic priest) and the last rites (confession and Communion administered to the dying). Luther denied the need for any sacraments but baptism and Communion; other Protestants have gone further in their denial of the importance of sacraments. Anabaptists accepted the importance of baptism but denied that it was appropriate for infants.

secular priest

an 'ordinary' priest such as one might find in a parish church. The term is used to distinguish them from 'regular' clergy who belong to an order, such as orders of monks or the Society of Jesus, in which members live according to a specific code known as a rule (hence the term 'regular').

separatist

a Puritan so disgusted by the failings of the Church of England that he or she decided to break away and set up a secret sect. Some separatists operated in England but many went abroad to the Netherlands and, in the seventeenth century, to America, to practise their religion unmolested. Elizabethan separatists are the forerunners of modern Congregationalists or Baptists.

surplice

a linen over-garment or tunic worn by priests while they perform their services in church. Surplices were deeply disliked by Puritans, who thought the clergy should not wear vestments associated with the Catholic Church.

vestiarian controversy

the debate that came to a head in 1565–66 over the vestments that the clergy should wear, especially the surplice.

via media

middle way or path; the Latin phrase often used both by historians and by people at the time to describe the path Elizabeth I tried to tread in her religious policy between different groups including Catholics, Puritans and reforming Protestants of varying degrees of radicalism.

Zwingli, Ulrich (1484–1531)

Swiss Protestant reformer and contemporary of Luther. Zwingli denied the Catholic doctrine of transubstantiation during the Eucharist, preaching instead that Communion was a simple commemorative act; he also denied the need for bishops and attacked the blanket imposition of fasting. Zwingli's ideas influenced Calvin and were also influential among English Protestants.

Timeline